The Conci Guide to t.. .... Angels

by Andrew Keeling

Edited by Mark Graham
A Spaceward Publication

Published by Spaceward, Cambridge, UK
ISBN 978-0-9562977-4-2

First Edition XIII/IX/MMXIII

Contents

Foreword
by Mark Kermode

We Will Never Give it Up

For the fans, the Comsat Angels were always Our Secret. From the red vinyl 7" single of Red Planet Revisited to the deluxe expanded CD re-release of The Glamour, the band's fortunes (critical and commercial) may have waxed and waned, but their importance to a core group of devotees never faltered. No matter how many concert tickets they sold, nor how many discs they shifted, the Comsats were never public property – there was something about their sound which gave the impression that these songs were for us, and us alone. Introducing the band onstage at Sensoria 2009 (one of the proudest moments of my life) I remember looking out at the gathering of the tribes who had made the pilgrimage to Sheffield - from the North and South of the UK, from France, from the Netherlands, from America, even some from Australia, a swarm of faces, all aglow, all at sea - and thinking that this was the biggest private party I had ever seen in my life.

One of the strangest things about the Comsat Angels' music was just how hard it was to describe in words. Rock journalists, falling at the first hurdle, would wrestle together phrases like 'cathedrals of sound' and 'minimalist song structures' before throwing their hands up in the air and admitting that you had to hear these records rather than read about them. The nod to JG Ballard in the band's name offered a clue to the sci-fi inflections of some of the lyrics, and the term 'cinematic landscapes' was frequently invoked – only by comparing them to books or films, it seemed, could writers begin to describe albums like Sleep No More, Fiction or My Mind's Eye. Even the great poet (and die-hard Comsats fan) Simon Armitage confessed that he found it nigh on impossible to transfer the experience of hearing Waiting For A Miracle to the page, although his terrific book 'Gig' expresses the impact which the band had upon him in terms which every fan will recognise as uncannily familiar.

What's fascinating about Andrew Keeling's intelligent and insightful work is that, unlike most traditional rock writing, it concentrates almost exclusively on the music, taking a serious scholarly approach to the apparently impossible task of unravelling the strange alchemical magic of the Comsats' sound. This is not a book about life on the road, inter-band rivalries, disputes with record companies, or any of the other ephemeral subjects by which rock writing is so often distracted. There is a notable absence of discussions about the Comsats' clothes, shoes, or haircuts – indeed, there is almost nothing about what they look like, only how they sound. Fittingly, illustrations of musical staves and 'dynamics diagrams' in this slim but deceptively detailed volume hugely outnumber pictures of the band.

By prioritising the complex, mesmerising sound which The Comsat Angels made over the white noise which sometimes surrounded them, Keeling manages to reassess their often undervalued role in contemporary culture, and to do justice to the extraordinary body of songs which the band created over more than three decades. This is a book written by someone who has listened to (and clearly loved) the Comsats with an intensity which echoes the passion of their most ardent audiences. It is an articulate and thoughtful expression of what it means to 'hear' their music, and an incitement (if one were needed) to go back and listen to those timeless recordings again. And again ...

Read, listen, and enjoy – but remember; they are still Our Secret.

Mark Kermode, August 2013.

1. Introduction

Recently I read Simon Reynolds's key document, Rip It Up and Start Again – Postpunk 1978-1984 (Faber and Faber). This, especially the Prologue, is essential reading as background for the following analysis. Although I enjoyed the book there was one glaring omission: it failed to make any mention of Sheffield new-wave band The Comsat Angels. Frankly, I felt this was an error of such glaring magnitude that I decided there and then to take it upon myself to set the record straight, so to speak.

I came across the Comsats during 1980 in the NME when their single, Independence Day was reviewed. Although I try not to buy records on the strength of reviews, on this occasion I did. Nor was I sorry. I bought their album, Waiting for a Miracle shortly after and in 1981 their second album, Sleep No More. These are both key sonic documents of those important times and beyond. At the time I was playing in a band and looking to change its direction. The example of The Comsat Angels was invaluable. Listening to those albums suggested vital clues as to how such a task might be achieved. I saw them perform at Manchester Polytechnic in 1981 sharing the bill with The Sound. In 1983 I decided on a course of further musical studies, left the band with whom I'd been playing and lost touch with the new-wave scene. In the mid-1990s I bought My Mind's Eye, the Comsats' eighth album and in 2006 bought the Renascent releases on the albums on CD. I was astonished to hear just how well the music had stood the test of time.

It may seem slightly anachronistic to be offering a traditional musical analysis of the music of The Comsat Angels using standard notation when the new-wave, or post-punk as it's often referred to, set out to rebuild an alternative scene by ringing-in the Postmodern era in the aftermath of the punk revolution. However, it's my view that the time is well overdue for a serious commentary on the Comsats who, in my view, were right at the forefront of the 1980s new-wave and beyond. I have decided to use language that I know to present what's there in the music, even though some might consider the method slightly elitist.

It is also my intention to show how this band seem to defy any attempt at mainstream classification and, therefore, can't for one moment be considered as one of the bunch from a period whose music has often received bad press. Only recently, with such bands as Franz Ferdinand, Bloc Party, Interpol and others citing the Comsats as a source of influence, can this be finally reconsidered. The Comsat Angels are, and always will be, worth more than that.

I would like to thank Stephen Fellows for going beyond the call of duty and responding to my many questions during 2007 and for also taking an active part in my alt-rock recording unit, Andrew Keeling and Otherworld – and even suggesting the name. It was from this perspective that I learnt conclusively that the Comsats possessed an exceptional talent. Also great gratitude goes to Kevin Bacon, Mik Glaisher, Andy Peake and Terry Todd for answering questions about the band. Thank you Mark Kermode and Simon Armitage for contributing to this writing. Thanks also to Alan Robinson for allowing me to refer to his sleeve-notes for the Renascent re-releases. Thank you Simon Robinson for the photos of the '90s Comsats and Jan Todd for the photos of the reunion tour. Appreciation goes to Nick Robinson for his essay on playing with the Comsats as well as to Tony Kinson for allowing the full gig list, on the Sleep No More website, to be included in this volume. All musical quotations by the band are reproduced with Steve's permission and the many quotes come from correspondence with him. Two full musical scores of 'Gone' and 'Sleep No More', from Sleep No More, will be included as part of the text, as well as 'Shiva Descending' from My Mind's Eye.

In April 2013 I sent each of the band members a list of questions as a way to get inside the music itself.

Kevin Bacon

A.K. Is there an identifiable Sheffield sound, musically speaking? Do you feel you and the Comsat Angels had a bearing in bringing that into being?

K.B. At that time in Sheffield bands didn't mingle – there weren't that many places to play. It was a dark time socially – without the networking. Strikes, power cuts, Thatcher. For at least the first year or so we wrote and rehearsed pretty much in a vacuum. Probably at that time the greatest compliment you pay any band was by saying how original they were. I guess you could say Sheffield was an anti-scene until the 80s.

A.K. What/who were your primary musical influences?

K.B. Mik, Steve and Andy. Then Pere Ubu. In my head, prior to the Comsats, Andy Fraser from Free. He was a great player, with his own space that he made. More importantly on their greatest hit, All Right Now, he doesn't play on the verses, comes in the chorus and then takes a solo. Genius. I've never been scared of not playing on verses since then. That's what I had in mind on Total War.

A.K. You've had a successful career as producer post-Comsats. Was the production one of your main roles in the band?

K.B. Kind of. I was just handy at processing our collective thoughts. I never said, "right lets do it like this". It helped us get there faster. In the studio with Pete Wilson I was probably a bit of an annoyance: "what's that, what does this do, can I try something"? Many times I've seen myself in others I've worked with and thought "oh my God that was me that was. Annoying."

A.K. How do you regard the mid-1980s period of the Comsat

Angels (Land and 7 Day Weekend)?

K.B. They were all right at the time. That's what bands did (pop) or you went on the dole. In retrospect they were on the whole disappointing with some nice moments. I learnt a lot. As I say, it was better than being on the dole. It did lead to opportunities that shaped the rest of my life – into production.

A.K. How much of an input did you have in the songwriting of the Comsat Angels?

K.B. Define songwriting? It worked like this, mostly in one of two ways:

METHOD 1
We jammed (for hours a day, every day Mon-Fri);
We all came up with sonic landscapes;
I specialised in brutal riffs – (Be Brave for example);
Mik bent time;
Andy freaked us out with the unexpected;
Steve would tape away – listening for stuff that got him excited;
Then at night Steve would retreat to his room and write a song over the top.

METHOD 2
Steve would write something up stairs and bring it down;
We'd deconstruct it and try and rebuild it in the most bizarre way we could;
Leaving just Steve's melody (Total War);
But in all cases Steve was the SONGwriter.

A.K. It strikes me that the Comsats were by far the best band of the 1980s and yet it seems success evaded you as a band. Why do you think this was so?

K.B. Luck, for me is defined as when Preparation meets Opportunity. We just never got the two synced up properly – others did.

A.K. Why did you leave the band post-My Mind's Eye?

K.B. What really happened was Mik left because there was nothing going on for months after recording My Mind's Eye. He was at a major low I assume. Mik won't mind me saying, but he blamed me for not being 'into the band anymore' coz I was off producing. He was kind of right. I was heading off somewhere else, but I had also just spent months engineering and mixing most of MME. I'd also come across someone who wanted to put it out. Mik wasn't much interested even when we got the release sorted.

Then one afternoon Steve called me up and said that Mik was coming back but only on condition that I left. It was hardly leaving as we hadn't played together or seen much of each other for months. Actually I was doing acid that afternoon (just a little bit) – and was thinking if I would suddenly freak out. When I put the phone down I just thought it was funny – but also there was a bit of sadness. The band had been everything to me for a long time and it had pretty much drained away – almost but not quite. Musically I didn't like the rocky take of some of the album. I don't like layered guitar and harmonies. I didn't like The Glamour much at all for that reason.

I went to see them with the new guys in the band at their first gig. I expected to be a sad but I was relieved not to be on stage – I would have hated it. Terry's a really nice guy but he swings on different hinges to me. He plays in a different way and for different reasons – and that's absolutely fine – no criticism – but seeing and hearing what I'd spent weeks tweaking and honing down to a specific thing changed into just bass was frustrating.

(On many records I've produced I've played bass. Finley Quaye's Even After All is really a Comsats bass line.)

Then they just slowly ground to a halt. I was so glad not to be there. The final gig in Reading (I believe) sounded like the lowest thing ever.

Years later I did it because I'd learnt to be very proud of what we did. I'd been producing records for twenty years with other people, I had a company with twenty young staff (AWAL) and thought it would be great for them to see what I'd done. Plus I just fancied it.

I went up to Sheffield for a chat and we ended up playing seven songs straight through. I think we all were really chuffed. I think me and Mik, by the time of the gig, had never played better. I played EVERY note as I had on the albums – not as I'd ended playing them live before.

I didn't want to do any more shows though. I hadn't time and the thought of (sorry for this) carrying my own gear and sat in the back of a van doing a drive back from Glasgow for a couple of hundred to a pretty small audience wasn't doing it for me.

The Sheffield gig cost me over £1,000 to do and it was well worth it. Trains, hotels, equipment hire. One of the best £1,000 I've spent.

I went to see them in London and I could feel that this was the last show they'd ever do. I almost went up to Terry and said "do you mind if I play the encore?" – but I didn't.

The Comsats still come up often. I was in LA at the offices of William Morris Endeavor (huge Hollywood agency) having a "getting nowhere" meeting with the head of music about something and I mentioned I was in a band – he asked – I said – and he leapt up and showed me his collection of our stuff. He pronounced "this is a gamechanger". Business flowed. Honestly it happens so much.

Pretty much everything I do now has its root back to the cellar rehearsal room were we spent '78-'81 or the experiences I accumulated along the way and as such I owe a huge debt of gratitude to the others and shall be eternally thankful.

Stephen Fellows

A.K. How do you view your work with the Comsat Angels, retrospectively?

S.F. Can I preface my answers to these questions by saying that whatever I say might be wrong - I'd suggest that I'm probably the least objective person in the world to comment on the stuff we did. That said, I hardly ever listen to our music - I'm more interested in going forward than looking back. But, if I force myself to answer this question there are two aspects - firstly, there's the music itself : we always tried our hardest, we worked relentlessly on our music, rehearsing/jamming/arranging 5 days a week, we were highly critical of ourselves and each other. When I look back I guess I regard the time we spent playing and working on the music as the best bit. The other aspect is associations that particular songs have with events at the time. This usually involves thinking 'if we'd only...' and ' what if ...' and is a complete waste of time! There's roughly eighty or so songs, probably more (I haven't counted them) probably a quarter or so were a waste of time - the rest I don't know about.

A.K. I've always been intrigued by the slight re-inventions in the band's music. Was this consciously done? Part of a modernising/updating strategy?

S.F. In a way, yes. We were always interested in doing things we hadn't done before, and less keen on repeating things we'd already done. Not so much modernising or updating as 'distancing'.

A.K. I always felt that the Comsat Angels provided the soundtrack for the 1980s and yet it's always bands like Joy Division who are cited as being influential. Do you find this somewhat irksome/unfair? It strikes me that somehow listening to the Comsats requires a different approach than listening to some of the other bands of the period i.e. musically and lyrically your whole approach was incredibly intelligent.

S.F. I don't really have an opinion about this. I wouldn't say we had any claim to 'soundtrack' a decade, after all our stuff wasn't widely known. I thought JD were great - well some of their stuff was; 'Disorder', 'Interzone' , 'Dead Souls' , ' Glass' , etc, etc. Peter Hook's bass playing was fantastic and is a massive part of what they did. It's the foundation which every other element rests on. If anything we tried to separate ourselves from what other bands were doing. It does make me laugh though when somebody says 'oh, this new band sounds like your lot', then I listen and it invariably sounds like JD - although the gloomy mood was perhaps something we had in common.

A.K. Did you feel part of the post-punk/new-wave movement? Or do you feel the Comsats stood apart from the crowd?

S.F. Well, we've been called various things - at the time it was 'new wave' or 'power pop' or ' goth' or even 'independent' - which was amusing as we were on major labels and 'banned' from the indie charts at the time. 'Post - punk' is a relatively recent term but I'm quite happy with that - it means that we came after 'punk' which is true.

A.K. The Glamour is one of THE best albums I've heard. How long did it take you to write it? I also know that My Mind's Eye is your favourite Comsats album.

S.F. Thank you. When you do an album (well, this is my experience) the 'machine' gets more and more 'cranked up' and efficient as you go along, so by the time you've nearly finished everything tends to be working really well - this is the point that the best stuff often gets done and it was why we carried on recording after the first version of the album was delivered. The Glamour flowed quickly and easily - even though internal frictions and relationships were difficult at times. I think we lost ourselves in the music as an antidote to the circumstances. I can't say how long it took to write - I always have a bunch of songs 'in the garage', that I'm tinkering with, and it's just a matter of seeing which ones work at any particular time.

A.K. I know you're working on a new album at this point in time (2013). Can you provide any hints as to its content? Have you played all the instruments on it?

S.F. After the band stopped I just kept on writing - it's hard to change a habit of a lifetime. Even when I was doing other things I'd relax by writing because I enjoy doing it. I suppose the 'pool' of songs that I chose the new album from contained some music that would have been worked on with the band if we'd carried on. Obviously it would be in a slightly different form because it would have been the band playing it. In my mind each of the songs on the new album is different to the others, that is, there is no overall 'style'. In the past I think the fact that it was all of us playing all the music gave it a kind of continuity. Strangely enough, now it's just me it seems more varied, but as I said earlier, I might be wrong. I play all the instruments, except on one song, ' It's Good to Be Alive' - on which my friend, Jim Wylie, invaluable production collaborator on this album   (without whom..), plays bass.

A.K. What are the other members of the band doing at the moment?

S.F. We are not in regular contact but as far as I know Kevin is currently in the States working for AWAL; Mik is about to move to the North East coast; Andy is working as a technician. Terry is working and playing with Frostlake (Jan, his wife, one of my oldest friends). I'm sad to say that Simon Anderson died yesterday (10th April 2013). He'd been very ill for a while.

A.K. Every now and then I notice the Comsat Angels mentioned in today's music press. It seems that you were fairly influential. How do you view today's music scene? Is there, in fact, a 'scene'?

S.F. Again - I don't know if we were influential or not. I wouldn't have said so myself. Today's music scene: from what I've heard I think there's less harmonic, rhythmic and melodic variation in today's pop music than there was before. I don't hear many great new songs but I'm very picky.

A.K. What have you done since the band stopped in the mid-1990s?

S.F. I left and the band stopped in 1995. I was working in Record Collector in Sheffield when the band folded and I carried on doing that. I really enjoyed it - I used to listen to everything that came in. In about Oct '96 I met Ian Ball who was a regular visitor to the shop. He was a member of a band called, variously, The Feelin' and Gomez, Kill, Kill The Vortex among other things. After I got to know the band I started working with them and became their manager the following year. This carried on until May 2005 when my contract wasn't renewed.

A.K. Were you surprised by the audience response to the reunion concerts in 2009? Do you think the band might continue at some point?

S.F. I didn't really notice the audience response - I was busy. I found the gigs hard work, not so much the playing but the social aspect. Also it was probably a mistake to do it without crew so we had to move our own gear. We were trying to save money. As I was recovering from major surgery this probably wasn't a great idea. I think I get a bit overwhelmed by all the people. My ideal situation would be to be wheeled into the gig in a flight case, get out of the flight case, do the show, then get back in a flight case. I think the only thing we could do now would be another album, but as two of the band have said they didn't want to do any more I can't see how it could happen. Also the economics of things has changed so much it would be impossible to do and have it make sense.

A.K. Which new bands do you like?

S.F. I'm not really into bands as such or any particular artist format. New to me - or recent? I do like some stuff by Tame Impala. I love Ariel Pinks ' Before Today' album, the new one not so much. I like Wooden Shjips. I really liked 'Lies' by Chvrches. It tends to be individual tunes really. I love Pyramids! by Frank Ocean. Also Phoenix, who've been around for a while but are new to a lot of people.

A.K. Mood X strikes me as being somewhat Krautrock/Brian Eno-influenced. Is this the case?

S.F. Possibly - I wasn't thinking of either particularly, although I do like a lot of that stuff - Amon Duul 2, Can, Ash Ra Temple etc. A particular favourite is 'Epitaph for Venus' by the Galactic Explorers, which is extremely 'spacey'. I love 'Apollo' and lots of Eno's other music. I really like Hans Reichel's playing - it's not conventional at all, that and the stuff David Darling did on 'Cello' maybe had more to do with it. There was a Small Good Thing album called 'Slim Westerns' that I really liked. Ry Cooder's soundtrack work also. The main thing about Mood X is that it's completely improvised. Some bits are improvised backwards and forwards at the same time. I've always done lots of improvising but rarely recorded it before. I did loads of recording just for the sake of it, around 15 hours, and it only became an album when Simon Robinson, who was running RPM records at that time, heard a bit of it and said he thought it might make an album. So I chose bits that I thought worked. I was originally going to call it 'Pornographic Galaxy' but no-one liked that title.

A.K. You were trained as an artist. How has this impacted on your musical work?

S.F. I wouldn't say I was trained exactly, although I do have a BA (ancient qualification) in Art & Art History. I'm not quite sure why I went to Art College now. I just seemed to be on that path. I could draw quite well but I spent a lot of time there doing music. I suppose it made me realise that doing 'art' of whatever sort can involve a lot of work and time to get it right. I always thought that my best friend was that little voice which says 'it's not good enough' - or maybe it was my worst enemy, I'm not sure now.

Mik Glaisher

A.K. Who/what were your primary drum influences?

M.G. Drummers on TV as a kid. Gene Krupa and then Ringo of course. Later on Simon Kirke, Bonham, Jaki from Can and Billy Cobham. So many and definitely too many to mention!

A.K. Did you have drum lessons or were you self-taught?

M.G. Self-taught.

A.K. It sounds to me that you're a jazz drummer. This certainly comes over in the rhythmic precision on Waiting for a Miracle. If this is the case, do you feel your drum technique was in keeping with the punk and post-punk/new wave ethos of the late 1970s/early '80s?

M.G. I would never limit myself to one style of music. I like to soak it all up and hope what comes out sounds like Mik Glaisher. You say I sound like a jazz drummer but I'd like to think I can rock with the best of them also! If all jazz drummers had been as loud as me then there wouldn't have been any jazz! In all honesty I thought the essence of post-punk was about innovation and creativity. That musical climate doesn't come along that often. Once you can pigeon-hole music and give it a name then it stops being original. So if you think my technique wasn't in keeping with those times then I'm glad! Another more succinct answer to your question is "No, I'm not a jazz drummer!"

A.K. Did you have any input into the actual songwriting in the Comsat Angels?

M.G. No.

A.K. How did the creative process work in the band?

M.G. Two or three different ways actually. Steve would often bring a song along in a more or less finished state and we'd stick some meat on its bones. Other times we'd completely deconstruct and rebuild it in that inimitable Comsat way! We also got some great results from jamming and often I would just find a rhythm which would form the basis of a new number.

A.K. The mid-1980s Comsats sound like quite a different band compared to the early period. How do you view this period in the band's development?

M.G. As one huge mistake really. We were out of a record contract and broke, then Jive wanted to sign us for a huge amount of money. We all agreed that we wanted more success than we'd achieved with the Polydor albums but as things unfolded we had less and less control over our music. I think we alienated many of our existing fans and failed to impress enough new ones. By the end of our disastrous relationship with Jive it was generally considered that the band had lost all integrity and was never really seen as the creative force it had once been ever again: it relegated us to a musical backwater from which we never recovered. There's a great line by Robert Redford in the film "The Natural" when he is asked about a previous girlfriend who shot him, he said "With some mistakes you never stop paying!" And that is how I see our time with Jive. Could I just say though that I thought Steve's singing on both Jive albums was exceptional!

A.K. Your drumming is very much different in the later Comsats. The rhythmic immediacy of My Mind's Eye and The Glamour is to the fore. Was this transformation mainly to do with the zeitgeist and changing fashions?

M.G. Yes, most definitely. The early 1990s were a great time for innovative guitar music and Steve was writing some killer riffs such as Demon Lover and The Glamour. I still believe that if The Glamour album was recorded by a new band in 1995 instead of it being a Comsat record dragging behind it all the baggage that that entailed then it would've been hailed as a classic!

A.K. How do you perceive the achievement of the band?

M.G. Oh dear! The hardest question of all. One of the most painful realisations to me is that, if I'm honest, the Comsats didn't nearly achieve enough. There was something monumental about the first two records, a real contribution to contemporary music during a very creative period in music history. We asked big questions about the way you can put music together; the collective imagination of the group was huge and the standards we set ourselves were so high. Essentially, every note or beat that interrupted the existing silence had to really matter or else it had no right being there. What we didn't play was as exciting as the stuff we included! With the benefit of hindsight, I could see a case for recording the first two albums only and letting history judge us on those alone. I felt we were untouchable after those records. People asked with incredulity how we'd managed to "distil" our sound down to those twenty songs and I guess the answer is through dedicated pursuit of a collective vision (if there is such a thing!). After that I thought we started to compromise left, right and centre due to forces both within and outside the group and so, as a result, lost our direction and focus. We seemed to be playing "catch up" rather than leading from the front as we had done on the first two records. In the later years, I felt we were seen as a "whatever happened to" band which I and I'm sure the rest of the group found very painful compared to how it was initially. But, back to your question. I think, at our best, The Comsat Angels created the most frighteningly original music of its or any other generation that influenced their contemporaries and new bands for years to come. It was an honour to work with such gifted musicians and I wouldn't have missed it for the world!

Andy Peake

A.K. It strikes me that the Comsat Angels were the best of the 1980s. Not only that, but probably one of the best. Period. How do you view the band's achievement?

A.P. Once we had evolved our 'voice' musically with the Red Planet EP, our collective approach to construction and arrangement around Steve's songs for what became Waiting for a

Miracle gave us a really strong working method and ethos for future albums. To me, the simplicity and minimalism of instrumental parts was intended to get to the core of the song and to evoke as much musical landscape as necessary in which to frame the song without overdoing it.

The Polydor albums encapsulated that approach and working with Pete Wilson, who just let us get on with it for the most-part, was a really creative time for us and produced some of our best work. However, frustration with the record company's total lack of understanding or motivation and their inability to 'shift vinyl' when it mattered had just about buried us by the end. We had press reviews most bands would kill for, but minimal sales. I also thought we should have toured more.

I agreed at the time that we needed to break out from our cult status, and our attempt to write more accessible radio friendly material with Jive did achieve a broader audience. To me, there were some great singles on Land and despite the radically different production we always had Steve's excellent songs to work with. I think we learned a lot but were led up some musical blind alleys here and there. Through the Island albums and beyond, especially My Mind's Eye, I think there is a real maturity to all the stuff we did.

The band's creativity, at its best, was always a result of our constant improvisation in the writing process with songs coming from either jams or fragments of songs that we jammed on, sometimes a whole song Steve had written and often taken into the studio with only a sketchy idea about what we would play on it. Having our own studio was wonderful, having the luxury of time to really get things right. Kev was also a top-class engineer by this stage, and creative with it.

Overall I think the Comsats were pretty consistent in producing some great original music and our combined individual styles and sensibilities as musicians were unique. I feel very lucky to have been a part of that and proud to have made albums that still stand up today alongside our musical peers at the time and have been influential for some of the bands today.

A.K. Your keyboard work is very distinctive. I hear your contribution as a soundscaper. How long did it take to come up with these 'ambient-like' arrangements?

A.P. I had been introduced to the VCS3 synthesiser while at Art College in 1973. I had no idea really how it worked but was blown away by the sounds it could make. I had heard the Minimoog on albums but never seen one close up. My onetime keyboards hero Keith Emerson seemed only to do about two things with it, one of which was running around with it on his shoulder! Art College in Sheffield had an early ARP synth and was the first one I played. I soon found that I was drawn to the noise generators and ring modulators as much as its ability to 'ape' other instruments.

Early days with the Comsats were severely hampered by lack of money. I finally got hold of a second-hand Mini Korg 700 synthesiser around 1978, the one used on the first album. I also started using guitar effects pedals. Fuzz, echo, chorus, flanging and ring-mod gave a whole new life to my then rather inadequate electronic piano and organ, always experimenting with where to place them musically alongside guitar, bass and drums.

Before samplers came along I had the idea of using 8-track cartridges, used then by radio stations and early car stereos, to pre-record sounds and noises for playing live, but this turned out to be a little impractical. I recorded the sound of scanning shortwave radio stations which we used in the middle bit of 'Monkey Pilot' and Sheffield's Castle Markets shoppers on 'Work'

I would have liked to pursue more Musique Concrete techniques. I had dabbled a bit at College using tape loops of the rhythmic sounds of presses and nail-making industrial machinery and the like, recorded then in the centre of Sheffield in now long-gone workshops and factories.

I tried to bring some tonal colour and more unusual synthesiser sounds into the music as well more traditional-sounding stuff, a big improvement in my armoury being the Prophet 5 which I started using around the time of the Fiction album. A five note polyphonic keyboard and some of the best sounds and ways of fiddling with them I had ever heard. I was particularly happy with it on tracks like What Else? Pictures and Nature Trails.

With the advent of samplers there were suddenly a million and one 'real' sounds available to us, the problem being too much choice in a way. I found it difficult at first to filter out the impressive sounding samples that come with the keyboard and are very tempting to use, although I have used some here and there, but then you start hearing them everywhere. Getting into programming them a bit more and recording my own samples made them more unique.

A.K. Were you classically taught?

A.P. I took piano lessons from the ages of about eight to sixteen with a local teacher in my home town of Grantham, with much encouragement from my father, a former military bandsman and double bass player in a dance band. He was also the choirmaster for our church and more of an influence on the classical side of my musical training than my teacher, a nice old dear who seemed to have switched off in about 1932. I finished with a Grade 8.

A.K. Who were your main musical influences?

A.P. As a child, I heard classical music and some trad jazz at home and of course the church music I was surrounded by at school, at church and at home. My father wrote and arranged masses and hymns for the choir, all sung in Latin in the early days but one of the most memorable things was hearing Gregorian chant sung in church, my father being a fan of it and having a fine singing voice himself. I still enjoy renaissance choral music, Palestrina, Tallis etc.

The Beatles were on the radio of course and I remember being impressed by Eleanor Rigby with its string quartet kind of arrangement, Lucy in the Sky, Day in the Life, Penny Lane etc. with George Martin's amazing arrangements. Psychedelia didn't really happen in Grantham (and I was a bit young for it) but listening back later to all the music I missed from that era was big influence.

I didn't really start improvising on the piano until about the age of fifteen, having discovered 12-bar blues and getting into Cream, John Mayall, The Nice, Deep Purple, Black Sabbath, Hendrix and Led Zeppelin. In my later teens I got into everything from Yes, Pink Floyd, Soft Machine, Free, Joni Mitchell, Steely Dan, King Crimson and Bowie to folk-rock, reggae and exploring 20th century composers such as Stockhausen, Ligeti, Stravinsky and

Ives.

The early Pere Ubu albums with the sonic contributions of Alan Ravenstine were a revelation as was Marquee Moon by Television, a lesson in how to construct powerful music with minimal instrumentation.

I had been interested in jazz in its various forms from the Mahavishnu Orchestra, Weather Report, the Miles Davis 'crossover' albums from the 70s and from about the mid 80s started listening to more jazz than ever. Bill Evans, Herbie Hancock, Coltrane, 50s and 60s Miles etc. all the great stuff really. I was also influenced by Steve Reich's Music for 18 Musicians and the other Minimalists; Philip Glass and John Adams. Catholic tastes. (ha ha!)

A.K. What keyboards/effects did you use early/mid and late Comsats?

A.P. The first electronic keyboard I bought was a Crumar piano in 1977. This was still in use on the first two albums. Using effects pedals made it sound more interesting though it was dire as an instrument. The first serious keyboard I bought was a Fender Rhodes but this had gone in part exchange for the Vox Jaguar organ and the Korg 700 by the time we recorded Red Planet.

Next along was a Roland SH-2 synth, used on Sleep No More and some other things, followed by an Oberheim OB-1 before I got the Prophet 5. The Vox Jaguar was replaced after the first album by a Roland VK-9 organ which had Hammond style drawbars and lasted right through all future albums. In fact I still have it. A Hohner clavinet was involved for a time: it's used on It's History, but went because it used to feedback on stage because we were so loud.

During the Jive period I used a Roland Juno-6, a cheap version of the Jupiter-6, along with the Prophet-5 and several other synths we hired in for the recording sessions, among them a Poly-Moog and Wave PPG. On Chasing Shadows I still had the Prophet-5 now with a Yamaha DX7 and afterwards an Ensoniq Piano as we were doing more stuff with real pianos on the recordings. Effects were now in rack-mounted units like a Yamaha Multi-effects processor and an E1010 for live work though I still used a fuzz-box and my trusty Electro Harmonix Ring Modulator.

By the time we were making Fire on the Moon, the Prophet-5 had died and I had the Emax sampler/keyboard, which was great value and relatively easy to program and edit. I still used the DX7 which was a pig to program.

Apart from using all these different keyboards, nothing compares to sitting at a grand piano for sheer all-round musicality!

A.K. What is the keyboard string effect you use at the beginning of Mystery Plane and All the Stars? It gives the music a truly American sci-fi feel?

A.P. Mystery Plane was a factory string sample and All the Stars a saxophone sample on the Emax.

A.K. What is your favourite period of the band, musically speaking?

A.P. The most successful albums for me were the first two, My Minds Eye and The Glamour. Fiction has some gems like After the Rain, Pictures, What Else? and Ju Ju Money. Land has some favourites for me too, I Know That Feeling, A World Away, Nature Trails and Shining Hour (though originally a B-side and created in a day)! 7 Day Weekend lacks a bit of identity due to the nature of its creation but High Tide, You Move Me and Close Your Eyes still sound good. Chasing Shadows sounded more like a Comsats album after the last two with The Cutting Edge, Carried Away, Flying Dreams and Lost Continent as my favourites. As Dream Command, Venus Hunter, Transport of Delight and Mercury still sound good.

Musically there is something from every period really. The time of the drum machine, the Jive years, was difficult for us in a sense, Mik being such a good drummer and although the ideas were his, just adding a few cymbals and overdubbing snare and toms here and there was frustrating, not just for him, and looking back, unnecessary.

Terry Todd

A.K. Who were your primary musical influences?

T.T. (As a kid in the sixties) Beatles initially and Kinks especially, getting into rock music in the late sixties/early seventies. Then bass influences were Chris Squire, Richard Sinclair and James Warren really, pre-punk just a total mélange of different musics and individuals, but I was just a bedroom musician in that period. The important thing about punk was just the idea that anybody could have a go and thankfully a lot of people did! I liked Colin Moulding's bass playing and Kev (Bacon) also had a definite influence with his playing of chords and open strings. Quite truthfully, I was just playing along to loads of records; riffing and improvising a bit made me ready to jam with other people. I mustn't forget the often overlooked bass playing of Paul McCartney, which is always interesting and inventive when revisited.

A.K. Were you always aware of the music of the Comsat Angels before you eventually joined them?

T.T. Yes, I saw them as Radio Earth once and as The Comsats a number of times. I think I first met Kev at a summer job in '78 and shortly after became friendly with Mik and Andy and used to see them down at Revolution Records (Castle Market) as well as at gigs when the Sheffield music scene of the late 70's/early 80's started to take off. I certainly bought the first four albums and singles and thought they were an important band in the post-punk music world.

A.K. Which bands did you previously play in?

T.T. '76/'77 - KID CHARLEMAGNE a club/covers band- a bit soul destroying but a learning curve!

'78/'79 -JUMP- I joined an existing band that played Feelgoods and Stax R'nB, but made it a bit punkier. I even wrote a couple of fast punky songs.

'79/'81- THE CHANT (formerly IVI)-melodic, slightly jerky...

probably Talking Heads influence.

'81/'85 – THE BOX- a rush of punk/funk/free jazz – first band on Godiscs!

'85 – THE WORKFORCE- Peel session '85/'87

'85/'87 – BONE ORCHESTRA – mainly acoustic...Tom Waits territory!

'87/'88- JASS- 12" on Waxtrax!

A.K. How much input did you have in the songwriting in The Glamour?

T.T. The songs were written by Steve. Once he presented the idea to the band, our input was arrangement and musical ideas. Within that it's hard to remember what was there to begin with and what was an addition! e.g. I can remember that little bass ascending part into the chorus of Audrey in Denim being played a few times at a rehearsal and Steve saying "keep that in"; and Andy playing with the chord progression from the end of that song in the studio and me saying that would make an epic outro. I assume this is how most bands work with a main songwriter and how you get a distinctive 'band' sound.

A.K. What was the main difference between the four and five-piece version of the band besides the personnel changes?

T.T. Difficult to say. We were still playing the 4 piece stuff successfully and maybe the new pieces became a bit rockier but that was the influence of the times and the way the band was writing and evolving.

A.K. Are you a guitarist by trade?

T.T. Not really, in that I've never made enough of a permanent living by it. I've done various jobs, record shops mostly, whilst enjoying concentrating on playing bass. I started by buying a cheap Spanish guitar and soon found that I mainly ended up listening and playing along to the bass parts of bands. I can play rhythm guitar but I'm lost on the intricacies of picking and stretchy jazz chords.

A.K. What have you done musically since the Comsats stopped in the mid-1990s?
T.T. '95/2000 – SOUP- with Mik, Andy and Simon, with Pete Hope (ex BOX) on vocals.

Then, a couple of benefit gigs with The Mysterons.

2007- played on 3 tracks for Martin Archer's In Stereo Gravity, and a track for The Army Of Briars CD. Did the pre-April 2009 Comsat Angels reunion gig rehearsals and then:

2010 The Last Weekend 'tour' with The Comsat Angels.

After that, to present day, jammed once or twice a month with Mik, Andy and Nigel Manning (sax).

2011- present day ORCHESTRA OF THE UPPER ATMOSPHERE the brainchild of Martin Archer www.discusmusic.co.uk CD just released with gigs on-going.

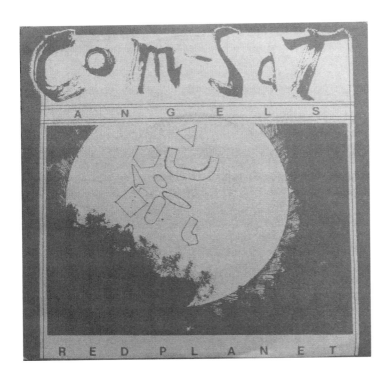

2. Beginnings

After early days at Psalter Lane Art College in Sheffield the pre-Comsats found themselves playing together as Radio Earth, a quasi jazz-rock outfit influenced by various old-wave bands. Stephen Fellows comments 'It was a very mixed up time musically. I was drawn to Hatfield and the North, Joni Mitchell, John McLaughlin, Frank Zappa etc. but me and the lads were enjoying XTC and the Stranglers as well, Elvis Costello and pop in general as always. We always listened to John Peel a lot. What we came up was mostly beyond hideous. There are also two late Radio Earth tunes on 'To Before': Tilted and Have You Seen. After one Radio Earth gig the promoter said he enjoyed it but hadn't realised we were a comedy band. Much as we all loved Andy's Rhodes piano we knew its days were numbered because the sound carried so many connotations.' The Radio Earth songs are stylistically muddled, looking back to Zappa yet looking forward to the Stranglers at the same time. Melodically, this is very different ground from the future Comsat Angels. I have already mentioned their response to the encounter with American new wavers, Pere Ubu. Fellows says, 'Even though they could be considered "arty" they seemed totally natural and uncontrived. We only had two or three tunes for a while and then they began to flow. I remember writing Waiting for a Miracle, Total War, Work and Postcard all in the same week.'

In the aftermath of the initial punk explosion those who were slightly older were trying to discover the way forward without regressing into what was considered the redundancy of old-wave progressive rock. Steve Fellows reflects, '1976-78 was a weird time. I still liked the music I'd liked before but it really did feel like something else was required. Punk wasn't it, though. We thought it was possible to have something that was more exciting but that was also musically interesting. I guess we were trying to do this as Skylids/Radio Earth – complex instrumental passages mixed with songs. There's one called "Bel Air Raid" that kind of almost works. I remember hearing a band called Punishment of Luxury around that time and they were interesting, also a US band called MX80 Sound who I liked a lot and still do. The Stranglers and the Costello lot (Ian Dury's band were prog stalwarts to a man) could obviously play, whereas the punks couldn't really do anything but play barre chords in a rock n'roll fashion and shout.'

With such influences from America as Television, Patti Smith, Pere Ubu and Chrome as well as those from the UK such as John Martyn and Richard Thompson, the band made their first self-financed single, Red Planet, in 1979. The three songs, Red Planet, I Get Excited and Specimen No. 2 are sophisticated punk or rather self-conscious post-punk exploring Fellows's favourite sci-fi influence. The song structure of Red Planet is interesting. For example, the shouted chorus which begins is segued into the sung verse. There are echoes of the Knack's single, My Sharona, with the octave leaping guitar and bass. Compared to later Comsats material another unusual feature is the F major key. Fellows notes that 'It was recorded in E, but speeded up, after mastering to F.' However, there are signs of what's to come with the tritone intervals in the main riff (see Example 1).

The middle keyboard instrumental hints at the huge musical reductionism going in the Comsats' musical arrangements (see Example 2). I Get Excited is Pere Ubu-influenced with punk-like vocals. The instrumental parts are more accomplished than those heard in punk bands of the period. It's also possible to hear the influence of Pere Ubu in the last song, Specimen No. 2, which was improvised in the studio. On the whole it points to the material found on WfaM with the Vox Continental's sound to the fore together with Mik Glaisher's tribal drumming.

First period – general musical features

The first period in the band's output demonstrates several well-defined musical fingerprints. First, there are the tribal drum rhythms drawn largely from punk but refined by Mik Glaisher's jazz style. Secondly, the bass guitar is often centred on repeated one-note phrases, although Total War, from WfaM, adds funk and lines build of dyads (two note chords), the latter used to heighten the arrangement. Thirdly, the guitar and keyboard solos are reduced to mere handfuls of pitches. There is no connection with blues-based techniques found in progressive-rock. Gone, from SNM, is a good example of both the guitar and keyboards. Instead, solos are often replaced, as in the title-track of SNM, with electronic gestures or, in the case of Total War, a dialogue between aleatoric (chance/improvisatory) harmonics and keyboard ring-modulation. Instrumental solos are placed in a way to enhance the sound-pictures the band were so good at creating. Expression outweighed superficiality and technique for technique's sake. Total War is an example of their ability to use overwhelming self-restraint in the service of the greater whole.

Vocals are usually short-phrases and gestural owing something to punk but also to Fellows's favourites Richard Thompson and Jimi Hendrix. Choruses are often fused to verses. One gets the impression that through the post-punk persona the more sophisticated jazz-rock and psychedelic styles show: Pink Floyd Piper at the Gates of Dawn-era and, possibly the Move. Harmonically, though, the Comsats steer well clear of punk territory. There is certainly not the harmonic sophistication of Hatfield and the North, say, as the band would have regarded that as outmoded and ponderous; nor is there the simplistic sonic/rhythmic gestures of the Buzzcocks. Instead, the innards of the music serve to create a commentary on the collective consciousness of the period. Others may have used rhetoric, but the Comsat Angels quietly got on with the job of creating great reflective contemporary music. Because their music may not have the extraversion of some others, the mass audience were, largely, to miss the point. It's as Fellows has recently reflected, 'People just didn't get it on the whole. I think I feel I have to be modest because the stuff we did didn't reach a wider audience.' This makes the Comsat Angels' musical contribution no less valid and, in a sense, highlights the contradistinction between mass and popular culture. The Comsats clearly fall into the latter category.

I will mention some of the musical enthusiasms of the band. These also illustrate the wider musical scene of the time. The first period demonstrates the influence of American new-wave musicians as well as artists from the 1960s. As I have said, Pere Ubu and Talking Heads were quintessential to the development of the band's early output. Stephen Fellows has also cited Patti Smith, Television, Frank Zappa, Jimi Hendrix, Todd Rundgren and Joni Mitchell as having an effect on him and the band. English underground musicians such as Richard Thompson, John Martyn, Robert Wyatt, early Pink Floyd, and the Groundhogs for the 'angularity of their guitar styles' have also been important. He also mentions the Beatles and the Shadows (particularly Hank Marvin). British new-wave acts also had an impact on the sound of the emerging band.

The English

Richard Thompson

Richard Thompson was lead guitarist with folk-rock band Fairport Convention, leaving the band following their Full House album of 1970. Thompson's clean Fender Stratocaster timbre was important in shaping Fellows's own approach to the guitar. For example, Thompson keeps guitar solos to a minimum in the service of a song. His use of musicians such as accordionist John Kirkpatrick provides a static harmonic basis to songs in a similar way to the use of keyboards in the Comsat Angels. The jagged edges in Thompson's style are given space to articulate the static sustain of keyboards in a similar way to the Comsats, providing rhythm and movement to the top inside parts in a musical texture, with a concentration on finger-vibrated, clean open-5ths. Stephen Fellows has commented that he 'became aware of RT's style around the second Fairport Convention album and has been a fan ever since. I saw the early '70s RT band three or four times. I liked his angularity and the strength, for me, of some of his melodies. You never quite knew where he'd go next which is always attractive. Actually, the beginning of Ju Ju Money (an early Comsats song later reworked for Fiction) is semi-nicked from RT. He's one of those who I hope was an influence but you never know. Thinking back it's possible Fairport as a band were an influence. Mattacks and Pegg were very tight, punchy and minimal. I mean, we all liked that stuff when younger; possibly I was the only one still listening to it. And Pentangle, I loved them.'

John Martyn

John Martyn was a stalwart of the English folk-rock scene from the late 1960s to his death in 2009. His many albums, such as The Tumbler and Solid Air demonstrate stylistic progression from, essentially, a folk singer to, latterly something quite difficult to categorise. His influence on Fellows and the Comsats is probably more in terms of the simple modal harmonic basis and rhythmic bass lines placed within the context of Echoplex effects, along with the short vocal phrasing: in Martyn's case, improvisatory, gestural blues. Such songs as the cover version of Skip James's 'I'd Rather be the Devil' demonstrate concurrent harmonic stasis and rhythmic movement, whereas the spacious 'Small Hours' (from One World) is reverb and delay-drenched. Similar effects are heard on the Comsat Angels' album Fiction. Their single, It's History, also uses an interesting triplet rhythm (3 in the guitar against 2 crotchets in the drums).

The Groundhogs

The Groundhogs were one of the most popular blues-rock bands of the late '60s. Their most successful album is 'Split'. Guitarist/vocalist Tony McPhee evolved a unique style unlike many of the other dominant blues players of the period. 'Cherry Red' is probably the epitome of this. In 'A Year in the Life', also found on Split, the guitar doubles the vocal line exactly, something that became a Fellows fingerprint from quite early on (see 'Map of the World' on WfaM). Textures are often bass dominated which is another Comsat Angels fingerprint.

The Shadows

The new-wave tended to look back to the 1960s and before to escape the direct influence and domination of progressive-rock. Several musicians from the 1980s have looked back to the Shadows, Stephen Fellows included. Another was Alix Johnson of Liverpool new-wave band Modern Eon. Hank Marvin's Stratocaster timbre provided a signal for many emerging guitarists such as Ritchie Blackmore of Deep Purple who is a self-confessed Marvin fan. The solo on Real Story, from WfaM, certainly pays homage to Marvin with its reliance on memorable melody rather than aiming at technical dexterity. Stephen Fellows has remarked, 'Not sure I was looking back, just that Hank Marvin was someone who made me want to play guitar. Some part of his style was always going to influence the way I play.'

America

Pere Ubu

As I've previously discussed, this Cleveland new-wave band probably had the biggest impact on the emerging sound of the Comsat Angels. Their 1978 album, The Modern Dance, includes fingerprints that the Comsats would eventually make their own such as Minor 3rd-based musical motifs, noise, gestural and pared-down drumming together with clean timbre guitar. They also dispense with long instrumental solos although, as Stephen Fellows notes, 'Untitled' on their Data Panic e.p. does have a longish solo. The song Street Waves, for example, begins with a noise element over the guitar riff which had some bearing on similar textures found on WfaM. In 'Chinese Radiation' there is some emphasis on guitar harmonics with a similar chord progression to the one found in 'Total War'. 'Life Stinks', with its bass introduction in Minor 3rds, must surely have remained in the mind of the Comsats, while 'Over My Head' has similar sounds to the ones heard at the beginning of 'Missing in Action'. The Modern Dance's back cover photo is telling with its image of Cleveland's industrial landscape possibly influencing the choice of cover photo for WfaM. Post-industrial imagery became a source of reference for several British post-punk bands.

Television

Marquee Moon, released in 1977, made a significant impact on the gathering momentum of the new-wave. Led by guitarist Tom Verlaine, Television was a four-piece from New York. The title track includes short gestural guitar motifs, pointing the way forward for Talking Heads forming from what has widely become recognised as the innovators, The Modern Lovers. Television's drummer, Billy Ficca, steered his technique away from clichéd drumming patterns heard in much progressive-rock. 'Elevator' also picks up on the chord shift I – IV which was something the Comsats would utilise on SNM. Their clean guitar style became an important signpost for other new-wave bands.

Patti Smith

New York musician and poet Patti Smith released the important Easter album in 1977. Smith felt the only way forward for her poetry was to place it within the context of a band. It includes Vox Continental keyboards and very simple poetry-based songs. The texture of 'Space Monkey' has some similarity to that of the Comsat Angels.

Talking Heads

Talking Heads' second album, Fear of Music, was released in 1979. Led by vocalist/guitarist David Byrne this album had a significant impact on listeners probably due to its nervous arrangements and funk-like guitar sound. It's also an observation on modern American life in songs such as 'Cities', 'Drugs' and 'Life During Wartime', a theme to which Byrne refers again and again. Harmonically, the songs are very simple relying more on stasis than dramatic shifts of key by giving space for the gestural vocals. The opening 'Air' exploits the I-VI chordal shift (F major to Db major). Fear of Music was also produced by Brian Eno and includes contributions from Robert Fripp. Talking Heads became a source of inspiration for the 1980s King Crimson on albums such as Discipline.

British close contemporaries

I will overview several albums of the Comsats' close contemporaries to discover if they share any common elements.

Joy Division

Closer was released in July 1980. The album is Ian Curtis's confessional. Musically speaking, there is tribal drumming found in much post-punk of the period as well as one-note repeated bass lines derived from punk. Joy Division always held tightly to their roots in punk. Closer, however, dispenses with conventional guitar solos. On the song 'Atrocity Exhibition' there is a free-form improvisation. 'A Means to an End' does include a Hank-Marvin-style clean solo. Synthesizer is used on 'Isolation'. The instrument was beginning to make its presence felt more and more during the period through the influence of the German band Kraftwerk and, particularly, through the work of John Foxx on his

Metamatic album of 1980. It's well know that Joy Division had been influenced by Foxx's work. Throughout the entire album there is a feeling of euphoric melancholy. 'Heart and Soul' has D-F natural-G bass riff introduction, although Stephen Fellows has said he didn't hear Closer until sometime afterwards and that 'quite a lot of SNM had been written by March 1980.' The vocal line has some similarities to the shapes used by the Comsats (see Example 3). The chorus also explores similar pitches (Example 4). And 'The Eternal' includes the definable introductory bass line (Example 5). The song is a dark, brooding soundscape which includes movement of chords over pedal pitches, something the Comsat Angels explored around the time of Fiction. Peter Hook's bass lines share something of the one-note style of Kevin Bacon's and is one of the sonic signifiers of their style, particularly their first album, Unknown Pleasures (1979).

Magazine
The Correct Use of Soap, Magazine's third album, was released in 1980. Its original and memorable music is an outgrowth from their previous album Secondhand Daylight. Song structures become more traditional and vocalist Howard Devoto folded the band after their fourth release saying they had nothing more to say. It strikes me that The Correct Use of Soap is a send-up album, with humorous dance and songs being central to it. 'You Knew Me' looks back to the 1970s. It includes some striking chordal shifts together with female vocals in the chorus (Ex. 6). The guitar work of John McGeogh is central to the album, with a Robert   Fripp-inspired   solo   in   the   song 'Thank   you (Fallettinmebemiceelfagin)'.

The Sound
The Sound toured with the Comsat Angels in 1981 and their third release, From the Lion's Mouth, is far in advance of the output of many bands of the period. The jangly guitars are part of the new-wave's style of reduction. There are also one-pitch bass parts, string synthesizers and a boomy 1980s production. The influence of Joy Division can be heard but the music is more dramatic with its minor key-based songs. The stand-out track is 'Contact the Fact' with its well-delineated verse/chorus structure. Skeletons is memorable for its tribal drumming, climaxing with the evocative coda where omitted syllables portray the skeleton subject of the song. The problem with the album is the keyboard timbre which gives the music a rather dated quality. Stephen Fellows remarks

that 'My favourite song is "I Can't Escape Myself" from Jeopardy. I did like Adrian's voice.'

PiL

By the time PiL's Flowers of Romance was released in 1981 some would argue that Public Image Limited were more or less a spent force. Fellows greatly admires the song 'Annalisa' from their first album. Flowers of Romance shows John Lydon's avant-garde side with its Captain Beefheart moments. 'Phenogan' has a feeling of the Orient to it and has a spacious quality to it. The title track named after Keith Levene's and Sid Vicious's former band is tribal and includes strings.

Gang of Four

The Gang of Four was essentially politically-motivated new wave four-piece using very basic harmonic structures. On Solid Gold, released in 1981, the music could be termed funk pointillism, or post-punk/nouveau funk, another style bands of the time engaged with as a way to escape the well-worn clichés of mainstream rock. 'Paralysed' uses i-VI (B minor – G major) chordal shifts, and 'What We All Know' includes gestural guitar, tribal drumming and falling Perfect 5ths in the vocal line at phrase endings which was something of a fingerprint for bands of the period.

The Cure

The Cure's second album, Faith, released in 1981 took its cue from Joy Division. 'The Holy Hour' is probably the best moment with its atmospheric keyboards and strummed guitar. The keyboard sound, though, is rather dated proving the point that technology has to be handled circumspectly if the music is to have longevity.

U2

U2's Boy, released in 1980, deals with innocence and experience through the eyes of a rather subdued and somewhat naïve Evangelical Christianity. The Comsat Angels toured with U2 during the early 1980s. Stephen Fellows: 'We did seventeen shows with them between 1-10-81 and 21-10-81. We didn't play the Sheffield show with them. They were worried that we would blow them off in our home town so they didn't let us play that one.' Fellows adds, 'This was probably a decision by their manager. They obviously didn't know Sheffield.' 'I Will Follow', the opener, is a key song with its extravert stance and i-bVI (E minor – C Major) chordal introduction. The interesting thing about U2's texture is the immense space opened up at the top and bottom of the texture with the middle occupied by vocals. There is certainly a shift away from American blues-based musics with many bands of the period. No less so in the music of U2 which, in turn, would become a blueprint for the new stadium rock of the mid to late 1980s and early '90s. U2 do, however, continue to look back to harmonic clichés of progressive-rock. For example, the E minor – D – C – B ground-bass heard on 'Twilight' one is led to King Crimson's song, Epitaph. Robert Fripp's guitar style was undoubtedly a source of influence for several new-wave guitarists. The falling 5th in the vocal of 'Twilight' is also heard (Ex. 7). And the semi-muted arpeggios which begin it (Ex. 8).

Durutti Column
The subsequent release to The Return of the Durutti Column is LC, the first to use a real drummer as opposed to a drum machine. Although Vini Reilly's vocals are included somewhere in the far distance of the mix, LC is essentially an album of fragile instrumentals, with infectious clean Stratocaster timbre placed in the foreground, delay-saturated textures and tribal drumming style of Bruce Mitchell. Guitar soloing is reduced. Musically, the entire album is a marvel, in particular 'Sketch for Dawn' and 'Sketch for Dawn II', the second including a verse and chorus structure. Never Known is memorable with its falling guitar lines and chords moving over a pedal pitch. Another of Fellows's favourites is 'Sketch for Summer' from the Return of the Durutti Column.

Siouxsie and the Banshees
When John McGeogh joined the Banshees in 1981 their overall musicality improved. The Comsat Angels also toured with them. 'Spellbound' is undoubtedly their best song from the period with its relentless chorus. Harmonically, the Banshees stick closely to their punk roots without any major melodic or harmonic innovations. 'Overground' demonstrates short vocal phrasing, but the use of chorus-driven guitar makes it sound central to the period.

Echo and the Bunnymen
The Bunnymen owe much to punk in terms of the short vocal phrasing and basic, chordally derived short harmonic riffs. They,

too, were very much part of the early 1980s and, as players, were non-technicians. In 'Stars are Stars' short guitar solos are involved and in 'Pride' the tribal drumming of the period is referenced. They were also part of the A Certain Ratio and Orange Juice nouveau funk movement and the deployment of I-bVI chording is often included in their songs. A large proportion of the songs from their 1980 release, Crocodiles, are in the minor mode.

Modern Eon
Modern Eon, from Liverpool, released Fiction Tales in 1981 and bears all the hallmarks of the period. In part, the album sounds like a reverb-drenched Shadows/Pink Floyd. The best is probably 'Childsplay' and the remarkable 'Playwright'. Essentially Fiction Tales is a concept-like album dealing with the fictions (persona) we create for ourselves. Some of the great bands often produce just one great album which sets them apart from the herd. Modern Eon's Fiction Tales is one such record. The removal of the 'prog-persona' was a key agenda for punk and new-wave musicians encapsulated by Robert Fripp's solo album Exposure (1979). The Comsat Angels' third album, Fiction, is also ironic in that sense.

The Teardrop Explodes
Essentially Julian Cope's backing band with a neo-psychedelic approach. Basically, Stranglers-influenced with clearly delineated verse and chorus structures. Kilimanjaro, the band's first album, includes the single 'Ha Ha I'm Drowning' with a falling Perfect 4th appearing at the end of phrases. 'Bouncing Babies' also includes the Minor 3rd at its root. 'When I Dream' sounds as if it could have been written in the 1960s. Brass arrangements are also involved.

John Foxx
John Foxx left Ultravox after Systems of Romance releasing his solo album, Metamatic in 1980. Featuring just Foxx on vocals and synthesizers with an occasional bass guitar, the album's jagged textures, Beatles-influenced melodies and electronica influenced a generation. Foxx offered a vision of a brave new world with 1984 only a breath away; a cold, grey, urban landscape populated by the 'quiet men'. This is a J.G. Ballard-like vision and a direct reaction to the counter-culture. Everything that came before had somehow to be washed away in favour of the post-Bowie world

thoroughly steeped in the modern. Foxx epitomises the Postmodern period with its jagged shapes and parallel lines, complete with the directness of Neu! and Kraftwerk. There is a parallel here with Minimalist classical music and the flattened-out textures of Steve Reich, Philip Glass, Michael Nyman and others.

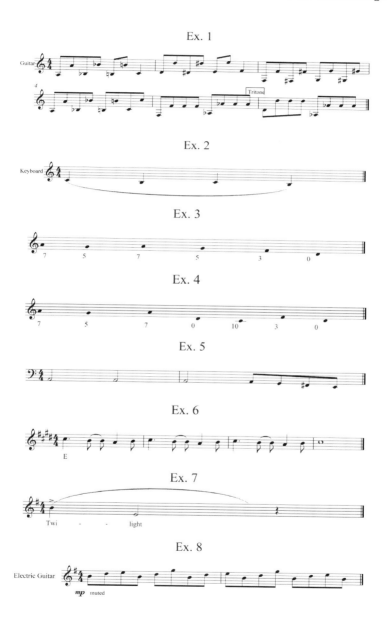

Ex. 1

Ex. 2

Ex. 3

Ex. 4

Ex. 5

Ex. 6

Ex. 7

Ex. 8

3. Waiting for a Miracle

Recorded in January 1980 but released in September 1980 to unanimous praise from critics and fans alike, WfaM was a hailed as one of the all-time best first releases from a young band. Including ten masterpieces of edgy, meaningful new-wave pop, and bearing many ingredients of the Comsats' sound, its use of metaphor such as war and conflict leave a long lasting and authentic impression of life in the early 1980s. The music conveys a kind of exhilarating desperation enhanced by the cover photo's post-industrial image of Sheffield taken from the motorway. For example, one of the lines gives a clue to its content: 'What kind of life is this?/It's in suspension/What kind of life is this?/Nothing happens.'

What follows is a track by track overview of the album.

1) Missing in Action
Beginning with half-bent guitar pitches suspended in mid-air. A subsequent accelerando and crescendo into the main rhythmic thrust of the song announces the sub-text of the album: 'Hello daily life/I don't want to fight today/I surrender/I'll put my toys

away.' The lyrics are supported by single sustained pitches over the battle-like snare-drum rhythmic rolls: G-B-D-B-G-E-D-A-G.

The modal key centre is E minor. Then, the first example of a Stephen Fellows fingerprint, where vocals are doubled exactly with the first guitar underneath (a technique first used on songs like Voodoo Chile by Jimi Hendrix and the Groundhogs). It fairly races along at crotchet = 168 with expressionless sustained accompaniment in octaves from the Vox Continental. This is a perfect musical metaphor for the no-place of no-man's land. The guitar is silent during the verse, providing great power when it is eventually heard (Ex. 9). There are two verses and choruses, the second chorus shifting-up and leading to an ascending guitar solo using 2nd and 3rd open strings, eventually bent up to a high F# with 2nd string bent up to 1st. This owes much to Hendrix's technique. It leads directly into chorus three where the guitar solo is eventually undermined by the keyboards. As an opener, this is blistering stuff.

2) Baby
Beginning with drums, the fingerprint Minor 3rd is repeated many times by the bass guitar (Ex. 10). It supports the lines, 'Don't want to be your baby/Don't want to have to call for you/It's not my fault don't blame me/I won't be crawling round anymore.' Up to here it's been in E minor mode with just voice, bass and drums using economy of means. When the full band enters at 0:42 it does so with great force. Comsat Angels' arrangements point-up maximum tension and dynamics are well-controlled to create listener expectation. The dramatic choruses of A and D/C# and A and D/G harmony outline a tritone shift. The stop/start vocal at 0:55 with the words 'I'm not/Trying/To run/Before/Before I can' over the original G-E-G-E bass line heighten the idea of the Chinese bound-feet in the previous lines, 'You wrap me up/Poor Chinese feet.' The simple, sequential guitar solo at 1:48 illustrates Stephen Fellows's Hank Marvin influence (Ex.11). The final exclamation, 'Baby!/Baby!' at 2:04 is the point of maximum tension reinforced by the sustained fuzz bass E natural, with ever-resent Minor 3rd included in the vocals as E-C# (Ex. 12). The song ends as it began giving the structure structural symmetry with the vocals placed distantly in the mix with the whimpered word 'Baby'.

3) Independence Day

Released as a single on July 4th, 1980 tribal drums and
harmonics are the sonic signifier of this groundbreaking music
(Ex. 13). Adding to the rhythmic propulsion there are extra
percussive effects from the Vox Continental at 0:07 and
elsewhere. Stephen Fellows says, 'Andy had a Crumar electric
piano as well which he used to put though an Electric Mistress
flanger and whichever boxes he had. That sound is him whacking
the keyboard. Another thing he did was whack it and twiddle the
ring-modulator at the same time, in the breakdowns in the title-
track.' The lyrics are full of 'ions': 'A declaration of the
intention/To stop extension into my airspace.' Fellows uses the
metaphor of conflict to celebrate a psychological state of
independence which, when it arrives as the chorus, is heard to
maximum effect. This music is celebratory; anthemic, even (Ex.
14). The vocals avoid the tonic E except right at the very end of
the phrase where the pitch is made into a lower neighbour-note
to the F#s. Up to this point the music sounds as though it's in B
minor but suddenly, at 0:30, for the second half of the verse a G
sounds low down in the keyboards. The written example bears
little resemblance to the aural effect of the chord as it actually
sounds on the record (Ex. 15). This is a mark of Andy Peake's use
of technical restraint during this period in the Comsats' output.
There is a subsequent shift to a D major 7th (Ex. 16). This soft
dissonance underpinned by G and D respectively points-up the
lyrics dried-out and brought into the foreground 'And I can't
stand up/And I can't sit down/Cos a great big problem stopped
me in my tracks/I can't relax cos I haven't done a thing/And I
can't do a thing cos I can't relax.' At 0:45 the drums intensify the
strophic setting of verse 2: 'You've got your habits/I've got my
customs/I'm sure you know it's got to be this way/No hesitation
and in the future/We'll celebrate on independence day.' Chorus
two intensifies providing great tension and release (Ex. 17). The E
centre is again avoided by dropping the G# to D and the tritone
has been transformed from its harmonic support heard in the
verse to the thematic material in the chorus hook line. At 1:37, the
main E modal centre is established by the loud fuzz bass
removing any harmonic ambiguity. A huge crescendo from 1:41 to
1:51 builds into transformed verse material (Ex. 18). The
subsequent chorus is the killer with the keyboards hammering
out dyads at the very top of the texture (Ex. 19). This is followed
by an economical, yet memorable guitar solo (Ex. 20). The final
masterstroke is the contrapuntal rhythmic vocal line shared by

Fellows and Peake at 2:50 (Ex. 21). Underpinning this is the Bacon-Glaisher pairing which owes something to the Wetton-Bruford rhythm machine of King Crimson or even the Andy Fraser/Simon Kirke rhythm section of Free. Fellows has said that band knew Bill Bruford's album Feels Good to Me which possibly had a bearing on the Comsats' rhythm section. And, of course, Kevin Bacon and Mik Glaisher have mentioned the influence of Free. This song marks the Comsat Angels as being leaders in their field.

Stephen Fellows has described the writing process in the band: 'We'd jam a lot...and I'd tape it and then go home and write stuff over what I thought were the interesting bits. I came up with quite a few of the bass lines as well, because they're critical to me. Like Waiting for a Miracle and Dark Parade, Be Brave etc. the very simple riffy ones. The tunes were often built on the bass lines so they had to come first. I can clearly remember exactly how Waiting for a Miracle, for example, was written. It was quite methodical. Kev definitely came up with the three semitone bass line in the breakdowns in Waiting for a Miracle.'

4) Waiting for a Miracle
The title-track is again in E modal minor. It starts with a memorable bass line, with Minor 3rds and Perfect 5ths outlining an E minor arpeggio (Ex. 22). The following vocal line has a similar intervallic structure, this time adding a rising Perfect 4th at the end (Ex. 23). The Perfect 4th becomes an important feature in the melodic line of the subsequent release, SNM. WfaM also introduces the anonymous he/she. In this case, 'She only has time for essential dreams.' The pre-chorus is the key moment in the song with its tierce de Picardie (sharpened 3rd) and Hendrix-like whammy-bar downward depressions extended by keyboard ring-modulation (Ex. 24). This is a key moment of Pure Comsat Angels magic, where the music is literally suspended by the use of noise which point-up the words 'What kind of life is this/It's in suspension/What kind of life is this/Where nothing happens.' The bass part adds to the dislocation in that it was later re-recorded. Stephen Fellows: 'I don't know why it was re-recorded. Maybe sound issues. Both phrases were one take. The second, after the bass had been re-tuned after I did the vocal.' According to Fellows the bass had been tuned slightly higher on the re-recording as compared to the original. Add the dissonant keyboard part to verse two's lyrics, 'It's party time at the top of

the hill/The air is freezing and the grass is like wire in between the trees' and a surreal landscape is created. The song, dealing with thwarted expectation, does have a sense of arrival in the delayed chorus at 2:05 with the words 'Waiting for a miracle/But nothing ever happens.' (Ex. 25). This also reintroduces the keyboard noise heard at the outset. The chorus is pushed to breaking point with eight repeats of the phrase.

5) Total War

Total War is a metaphor for a relationship issue. It begins with a war-like marching drum part. Using a slow portamento keyboard part, it culminates in two bell sounds on beats three and four of the bar issuing a warning of the vocal entry based on the fingerprint Minor 3rd (Ex. 26). The vocal part is layered over the top of the percussion and keyboard part (Ex. 27). The impression is one of a couple confidently striding down the street suggested by the accenting of every beat of the bar, with strong accents on the word 'the' and other unimportant words. The keyboard bells, combined with vocals alone, articulate the posturing of the song's anonymous protagonists. Another aspect of absence is the silent guitar, the drums and vocals providing the entire foreground. Stephen Fellows has said 'Mik (Glaisher) was great at "deconstructing" rhythms. Total War was a straight ahead rock song until he had the idea of slowing it down and playing a beat inspired by Devo's version of Satisfaction.' The bass enters on the upbeat to the second half of the verse always providing a kind of walking rhythm. It's also less four-square but includes the Minor 3rd fingerprint (Ex. 28). The reduced keyboard further compounds the falsity of the pose (Ex. 29). The rhythm becomes more regular but no less tribal at 0:33 with the words 'You don't like my friends/You don't like my clothes/You think that I'm crazy/Any other girl would just pass over.' This is accompanied by the banal harmony vocal (Ex. 30). Verse two is even sparser. Now the bass sustains an A 5th under the words which emphasise the war theme of the song, pointing-up the isolation in the lyrics, 'Nothing ever comes between us/In no-mans-land the danger zone/Look at us pick up the pieces/We live together on our own.' The chorus is held back till 1:44 and here, for the first time, the important hook-line is heard (Ex. 31). At 1:56 the chorus provides the first indication of a straight 4/4 rock rhythm, but not for long: at 2:02 there is an A 5th sustain for four bars in the bass with a very soft ascending, ring-modulated portamento in the keyboards with a bell sonority on the fourth bar of the coda. This is the masterstroke of the song with its doomy, cutting, yet meaningful bass line (Ex. 32). The bass goes on to underpin the chorus (Ex. 33). The keyboards portamento descends and the drums provide the strong rhythmic backdrop reviving the impression of Andy McCullough's kick-drum work on King Crimson's Lizard, but here with greater textural economy. The guitar harmonics play in dialogue with the noise keyboards. Total War brings side one of the original vinyl to a close.

I will overview the second side of the album. Very often a CD does not fully do justice to the original vinyl albums where songs were placed in important places for maximum listener impact. The break between side one and two allows for this in a similar way to intermissions in classical music concerts.

6) On the Beach
Inspired by Neville Shute's book, and placed at the beginning of side two, On the Beach comes as a complete change of mood. It is in D mode and with a subsequent harmonic shift now outlines a retrograde Minor 3rd to B. The chorus reintroduces the G–E shift fo the words 'Here comes a great big wave.' The guitar chord is spread to allow for the ringing open fourth string to sound. Fellows has said that he uses open strings to allow for resonance (Ex. 34).

7) Monkey Pilot
A World War II metaphor, this time centred on control – and being out of control. The song begins with clean guitar in open 5ths doubled by the bass an octave lower. The rhythmic groupings are interesting in that the sequentially repeated grouping, beginning on C, fall on beat three rather than beat one of the original D groupings (Ex. 35). The powerful attack of the vocal entry together with the full band emphasises the line, 'Sometimes I feel/Out of control.' The mention of the monkey pilot is left until the very end. Verse one's lyrics are telling with the descriptive metaphor of the cockpit. The drums take the out-of-control-ness one stage further by using the rhythmic material of the opening to accompany the verse lyrics at 0:30 (Ex. 36). Word-painting is the key to the song with the climbing vocals of 'Sometimes I feel/Like a monkey pilot' during the static section prior to the powerful final chorus. This is an example of the artist's eye which epitomises all of Stephen Fellows's writing.

8) Real Story

Commentators feel that Real Story is one of the Comsat Angels' strongest songs, probably for its lyrical and musical directness. Essentially it deals with the fictions of unreality, whether it be addiction, religious fundamentalism or political manifestos. For example, the protagonist of the song is cited as being 'Now he's in unreal estate/Until he dies.' The strength is provided in the 'unreal' key of Eb minor (Ex. 37). The keyboards add colour in open 5ths at the top of the texture at 0:23 (Ex. 38). This prepares for the entry of the words of verse one which spat out venomously: 'Is it some kind of stupid joke/The fiction that he speaks.' The concept of fiction is something Fellows was to return to during the later third album. He has recently said, 'I've never enjoyed written fiction that much because, as we know, life doesn't have a plot, or a narrator, and it rarely makes sense.' The hammered chorus has clipped and single dyads in the guitar part and the guitar solo is highly effective (Ex. 39). At the back of the Eb-Gb minor key, the Minor 3rd is always present in the bass guitar.

9) Map of the World

A tritone away from the Eb minor of Real Story and totally different in character, Map of the World is a Beatles-like pop song with a killer opening guitar riff (Ex. 40). The song is in A major and is a fine example of the Fellows fingerprint technique of doubling a vocal line with the guitar an octave beneath. The melody line also outlines the tritone, C#-G (Ex. 41). Of all the songs included during the early period of the Comsat Angels' output, this one demonstrates their accomplished musicianship. Mik Glaisher's drumming, from 1:52 onwards, is superb and the final chord brings to mind the Beatles's Help! Altogether, Map of the World is a brilliant evocation of useless information conveyed by the metaphor of a map.

10) Postcard

The final Postcard reintroduces the Minor 3rd, now A-C, as a dark keyboard sustain with evenly treading crotchets over the top. Beginning from the early sketch, Living In, this song has menace in abundance in its accumulative structure, preparing what was to come on SNM.

Ex. 14

Ex. 15

Ex. 16

Ex. 17

Ex. 18

Ex. 19

Ex. 20

Ex. 21

Ex. 22

Ex. 23

Ex. 24

Ex. 25

Ex. 33

Ex. 34

Ex. 35

Ex. 36

Ex. 37

Ex. 38

Ex. 39

Ex. 40

Ex. 41

4. Sleep No More

Stephen Fellows has said that SNM, compared to WfaM, was a sort of 'refined and pared-down and louder version, much less poppy, more brutal, less fancy, and in a way hopefully more sophisticated...less is more or something like that.' The album was originally to have been called Light Years, but on hearing that the Electric Light Orchestra had an album release with a similar title, Sleep No More was felt to be more appropriate. The album was released in 1980.

Fellows went on to say 'the concept was the sound picture rather than one involving "meaning" as is more traditional. There's a lot of anger on this album that I didn't notice at the time. Maybe it's our punk album in a way. The other thing about the material is that the individual parts got even simpler. An example is the chorus of the final song, Our Secret which is basically D sus4/E. We were developing individual signatures as players.' It also strikes me that SNM is a shift away from the visible northern industrial landscapes of WfaM to inscapes of the collective consciousness of the period; the collective unconscious, even. It touches the existential nerve of the time and in doing so is the soundtrack par excellence to the early 1980s.

Basic structures

SNM, on the whole, is in E modal minor, with a dip to D for the song, Dark Parade, followed by a balancing ascent to G and Eb for Light Years and a resolution to E minor at the end. The decision to follow this key scheme was, according to Fellows, '...conscious, in that the sustained guitar part (on the track SNM) was nicked from Daevid Allen (of Gong) and is open strings at the twelfth fret so...resonance as well. And I wasn't that good at singing and playing at the same time, so the more open strings made things easier to play without looking down. With Dark Parade we wanted the subterranean low D which wasn't that common at the time. Kevin had just got a Hipshot detuner which allowed instant and accurate detuning. The album wasn't really conceived as a whole, but it was sort of obvious what should go where. We were fully aware it wasn't an easy listen. We also sort of realised that you could vastly increase the potential for tension and power if you weren't banging away all the time. Contrast is a powerful tool.'

The contrasts of SNM are many, but the element of restraint in service of the greater whole is possibly one of the album's lasting strengths. Young players often go overboard with technique. However, here the result is quite different.

Instrumentation

An entire book could be presented about the use of keyboards in bands from the 1960s onwards. The 1970s alone produced excessive interest in keyboards and keyboard playing as technology developed, prompted by the needs of the players themselves. During the 1980s new-wave bands rejected such instruments as the mellotron and the Moog synthesizer as they were too much identified with progressive-rock. I wonder if music of the 1980s has had something of a bad press for the rather monochrome sonority of the Roland DX7 which, in turn, became identified with the evolving excesses of style over content in music in the middle of the decade. The Comsat Angels' use of Vox Continental organ, with devices such as flanger and ring modulator, means their early period has held up particularly well.

Secondly, at this time Stephen Fellows's guitar timbre was shorn of the familiar 1980s Roland Jazz Chorus effect. A clean

Stratocaster timbre, with reverb is the overriding guitar sound on the first two albums. Guitar solos are also kept to a handful of pitches. Exploring open-strings and arpeggiated chording, Fellows's style synthesises the concerns of Hendrix, Richard Thompson and Hank Marvin without sounding like any one of these. One particular solo is Diagram (track six of SNM) at 3:00. It sounds as if it may have been influenced by Robert Fripp's solo on Easy Money from King Crimson's Larks' Tongues in Aspic (1972). Fripp is regarded as an important part of the post-punk period through his work with David Bowie, Brian Eno, Blondie and Talking Heads after moving to New York in 1977. His solo album, Exposure (1979), is stripped of techniques found in King Crimson's earlier output. Stephen Fellows says he has seen every incarnation of King Crimson and particularly liked Fripp's work with Brian Eno on No Pussyfooting (1971). On SNM, the guitar as a rhythm instrument is restricted to providing jagged rhythmic arpeggiations within the framework of the ambient-like keyboards. The title-track sustains a long E-A-D-G-B-E harmonics aggregate at the 12th fret with bottleneck, meshed with the keyboard harmonics produced with weights on the keys while manipulating the drawbars.

Bass and drums provide strong rhythmic momentum in a similar way to Wetton and Bruford of King Crimson 1972-74, although the Comsats' rhythm section shows a greater affinity with the reductionism of the new-wave. The bass often repeats small collections of pitches as moving pedals; Bacon's slap style (although restricted to one or two places) and glissando is heard on Restless. Glaisher's fills on Our Secret point to his interest in jazz-rock. The vocals, which on WfaM are sometimes imbued with something of punk's abrasive attitude, are here placed some way back in the mix and fairly expressionless throughout.

Dynamics

A further aspect of the Comsat Angels' musicianship which requires exploration is dynamics. Track one of SNM, Eye Dance, is a good example of a band who make use of this aspect to point-up psychological states or otherwise. Eye Dance is about an emotional connection between two people. Diagram 1 charts the placing of dynamics in relation to structure. The trajectory was clearly conscious as Fellows has previously stated (see Diagram 1).

Harmony

I plan to discuss harmony and intervallic structure as both open a window on the character of the music under discussion. U2's Bono described the music of the Comsat Angels as having a 'terrible beauty' and Stephen Fellows has recently described it as having 'ecstatic melancholy.' This may refer to the abundance of Minor 3rds which permeate the album both melodically but, more particularly in harmonic terms.

The ten songs of SNM demonstrate how Minor 3rd-related harmony provides a structural backbone for the album as a whole. The Minor 3rd was used to great effect on WfaM. In SNM it is more or less everything. The interval of the Minor 3rd is something used in many folk traditions, but particularly the English. It could be that the Comsats were effectively engaged in creating a modern industrial folk music of sorts, although this was probably at an unconscious level. Stephen Fellows has an admiration for folk artists such as Martin Carthy and Clive Palmer. Minor 3rds were used for melancholic 'affect' during the Baroque period of the sixteenth and seventeenth centuries in works such as Henry Purcell's anthem Hear My Prayer. The harmonic shift a major third from E minor to C major, at the back of Eye Dance from SNM, probably goes back to the same shift heard in Eleanor Rigby or, even, Nothing More by Fotheringay. 3rds effectively quarter the octave (i.e. E-C-A-F). On SNM the eventual appearance of G major, in Light Years, is a Minor 3rd from the E minor which, up until that point, was the predominant harmony. Just as the ear becomes accustomed to this new key – the relative major – G is used as a pivot pitch into the subsequent Eb major (G is the third of Eb) which comes as something of a surprise. This shift provides balance for the E minor – C major shift in a song such as Eye Dance. It is also heard on the title-track. The conflict of major and minor heightens the tension which symbolises the inner, invisible conflict at the heart of SNM. Resolution arrives in the tenth song, Our Secret, marking a return to the tonic E minor (see Diagram 2).

Melodic motifs and intervallic structure

Stephen Fellows has commented that 'Melody is where it's at for me, but the fascinating thing is that it can be very minimal, almost non-existent, but still very strong. I do worry about whether or not some of my florid ones are cheesy or not. I've always heard Arvo Part as melodic, particularly something like Adonai from the Seven Magnificat Antiphons, or the loud bit in Miserere about ten minutes in. Or the beginning of Passio or Cantus.'

There are four main types of melodic motifs associated with intervals at the back of the album: a) rising and falling semitones (Minor 2nds); b) Minor 3rds; c) Perfect 4ths; d) Perfect 5ths. I will discuss each.

a) Rising and falling semitones/Minor 2nds.

These are heard at the outset of Eye Dance (they may exist as an unconscious musical metaphor for the dancing eyes of the song) and are often realised in the guitar and keyboard parts (Ex. 42). A longer, more complete use of the interval is hear in the brooding coda of Restless where the guitar plays a low E-F drenched in delay (Ex. 43). The last example is also found in its original form in the guitar solo (middle 8) of Be Brave, as part of a downward bend (Ex. 44). In this way the guitar coda of Restless is the retrograde version of the original and may be a metaphor for what Fellows has recently divulged as the meaning of Light Years: 'Light Years...as you know a light year is the distance light travels in a year, so I'm using it as a metaphor for "unrecoverable" time.'

Goat of the West also involves a rising semitone (Ex. 45) as does the end of Our Secret (Ex. 46 and 47). It also occurs in Gone (Ex. 48) as well as in Diagram (Ex. 49). Perhaps the rising semitones refer more to optimism: in the context of Eye Dance, the recollection of a moment of enchantment; as the hope in Our Secret; the moment of realisation of disbelief in Goat of the West? The falling semitones may represent the pessimism felt in Be Brave.

Minor 3rds

The numerous examples of Minor 3rds may be symbolic of what Stephen Fellows has referred to as 'ecstatic melancholy' present on the album. As I have discussed previously the Minor 3rds, as well as being a recognisable Comsat Angels fingerprint, connect WfaM with SNM. Be Brave is the song that hammers home the interval, first in the bass as a Minor 10th (compound Minor 3rd)

(Ex. 50). The opening vocal line also includes it (Ex. 51). Perhaps the Minor 3rd is a symbol for the 'whispering at the back of everything' as the lyrics state in the song. It is also transformed into its retrograde form in Gone (Ex. 52). Dark Parade, often referred to as the Comsats' epic, is predominantly underpinned by the bass guitar Minor 3rd D-F (Ex. 53) and is also hammered home in the vocal part (Ex. 54). The chorus of Diagram also includes the interval (Ex. 55). It is on Our Secret which includes the summation of the interval in the bass part both in its linear and vertical forms (Ex. 56). The rising semitone and the Minor 3rd are combined in this final song as if to emphasise both optimism and ecstatic melancholy.

Perfect 4ths
There are many examples of mainly rising Perfect 4ths in the thematic material (Ex. 57 and 58). These two examples, from the Eye Dance and the title-track respectively, are motivically identical and create unity between the two songs. They also show that the Minor 3rd is connected by an A natural neighbour-note, as well as the Stephen Fellows melodic 0-5-3 fingerprint: E-A-G. These 4ths also create a 4-3 suspension by resolving from the dissonant A natural to a G natural, the third of an E minor triad. Be Brave also includes the Minor 3rd and the Perfect 4th (Ex. 59). Gone also includes the Perfect 4th as part of a longer line (Ex. 60). Dark Parade includes the interval in descending form (Ex. 61). Goat of the West has a falling 4th as part of the Minor 3rd/Perfect 4th motif, derived from the motif of the longer line of Eye Dance and SNM. Here, though, it's re-ordered (Ex. 62 and 63). The example from Goat of the West illustrates Fellows's very short thematic gestural phrasing which is possibly the outworking of his enthusiasm for Jimi Hendrix and Richard Thompson.

Rising and falling Perfect 5ths
There are many examples of the 5th in the thematic material of bands of the post-punk period. Echo and the Bunnymen's music immediately springs to mind. SNM features the interval but its inclusions are more subtle than some other post-punk bands. The vocal line in Gone, from 0:30 onwards, can be reduced to a falling, filled-in Perfect 5th (Ex. 64). Dark Parade's verses also feature a decorated rising 5th towards the instrumental refrain at

the end of each verse (Ex. 65). In Goat of the West, the fall of the 5th precedes a rising Minor 3rd. Pitch-classes here are 7-7-0-3-3-2-2-0 (Ex. 66). The most explicit use of the interval is found in the bass part of Our Secret as if to emphasise the use of both the 5th and the Minor 3rd (Ex. 67).

Texture

The score of the title-song (see appendix) has something of the look of 1980s Minimalist contemporary classical music. It is spacious without pop music's predominant use of verse and chorus structures. There is also something of Arvo Part's style here and Stephen Fellows has spoken about his enthusiasm for Part's music. Part was influenced by the aleatoric techniques of John Cage. Economy of means was a key element in avant-garde music of the 1980s and no less in the new-wave as in the 'holy' minimalism of Part, Tavener and Gorecki. (Also see Diagram 3).

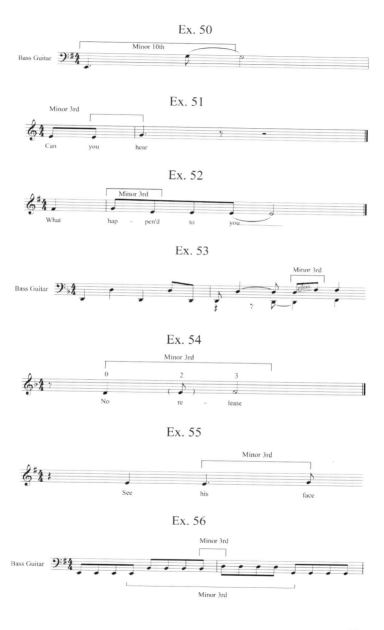

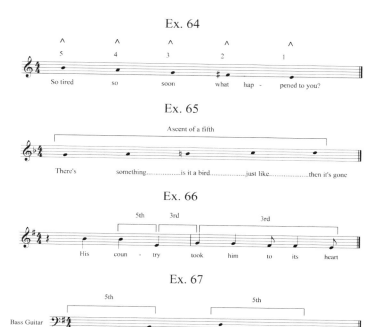

DIAGRAM 1

EYE DANCE – DYNAMICS

| 0:29 | 1:21 | 1:47 | 2:00 | 2:26 | 2:58 | 3:37 |

INTRODUCTION — VERSE 1 — CHORUS — INTRODUCTION — VERSE 2 — CHORUS - extended — CODA (INTRO EXTENDED)

(ff) FULL BAND

(mf) REDUCED – i) GUITAR MUTED
ii) KEYB. ON BEAT 4
PLUS VOCALS
INSTRUMENTAL

(f) GUITAR – OPEN CROTCHETS
KEYB. – SUSTAINED CHORDS
ii) BASS – QUAVERS

(ff) FULL BAND
INSTRUMENTAL

(p) FULL BAND – i) GUITAR – SUSTAINED CHORDS INTO ARPEGGIOS
ii) KEYB – ON BEAT 4
iii) BASS – SOFTER
iv) DRUMS – SOFTER/LESS ACTIVE
PLUS VOCALS
Part of GOLDEN SECTION (2:0738)

(f) FULL BAND

(ff) GUITAR: AS IN INTRO THEN IN 4ths
ii) ENDS OF CLIMACTIC WASH RHYTHM
INSTRUMENTAL

ff
f
mf
p

DIAGRAM 2 — HARMONY

SIDE 1.

EYE DANCE	SNM	BE BRAVE	GONE	DARK PARADE
v. E minor mode Em — C Major 3rd Ch: Em — C Major 3rd	E" (piled up 4ths) Em — C m3 major 3rd Em	v. Em mode m3 Ch: D–C–A/G D–C–A/E /G	v. Em mode m3 D B A G /E /E /E /G MIDDLE 8 B–D– m3 C# v. Em) m3	Dm mode End of verses F – Am7 – D" m3

SIDE 2.

DIAGRAM	RESTLESS	GOAT of the WEST	LIGHT YEARS	OUR SECRET
Em mode	v. Am – C m3 Ch: G – D	v. Em mode Em/G – Am Ch: Em Gm/G – D	INTRO – G major ......pivot verse: Eb – F – G/G – F/G – F – Eb major 3rd	INTRO – Em – G m3 v. Em9

DIAGRAM 3

1) EYE DANCE (3:37) 2) SNM (2:50) 3) BE BRAVE (4:04) 4) GONE (3:24) 5) DRAG PARADE (5:02) 6) DIAGRAM (3:40) 7) RESTLESS (3:12) 8) GUNT OF THE WEST (3:12) 9) LIGHT YEARS (4:21) 10) OUR SECRET (4:06)

	1) EYE DANCE	2) SNM	3) BE BRAVE	4) GONE	5) DRAG PARADE	6) DIAGRAM	7) RESTLESS	8) ANGER – OBSERVATION	9) LIGHT YEARS	10) OUR SECRET
a) CHARACTER / ENCHANTMENT	SOUND-PICTURE		MENACE	LOSS	OBSERVATION	RESOLUTION	LOSS OF BATTLE	ANGER – OBSERVATION	UNRECOGNISEABLE TUNE	HOPE
b) TONALITY	Eb" – C	Eb" – C (minor)	Eb mode	Eb mode	D minor mode	Eb mode	Am mode	Em mode	Intro: G# / V: Eb – G – C – F / Bb Eb	HOPE
c) MOTIFS	*(handwritten musical notation & motifs)*									
d) TEMPO	♩=138 FAST	♩=144 FAST	♩=132 FAST	♩=126	♩=112 MODERATE	♩=120 MODERATE	♩=63 SLOW → ACCEL	♩=120 MODERATE / ♩=63	♩=63 SLOW ACCEL	♩=116 MODERATE
e) TEXTURE	FULL / SERIOUS REDUCED VARIABLE	FULL SERIOUS – FULL	FAST RALLENTANDO	FULL	REDUCED TO FULL	FULL	REDUCED	FULL	FULL / VARIABLE	FULL / VARIABLE
f) DYNAMICS	mf	f VARIABLE	f VARIABLE	f VARIABLE	mp	f – mf	mp	ff	mp → ff → FADE mp → f → FADE	
g) STRUCTURE	VERSE/CHORUS STROPHIC	VERSE/INSTR. STROPHIC	VERSE/CHORUS STROPHIC	VERSE/MIDDLE	VERSES	VERSE/CHORUS	VERSE/CHORUS	VERSE/CHORUS/CODA	VERSES	VERSE/CHORUS STROPHIC

5. Fiction

Following SNM the band wrote and recorded their third album, Fiction (1982). In the sleeve-notes to the re-mastered edition (Renascent 2006) Stephen Fellows said he didn't want to make 'another record as intense as SNM...it was so dark that I felt it skewed things a bit – possibly even mentally for me. I just felt if we carried on going in that direction it'd lead to madness or maybe something worse. I think the new vibe (for Fiction) came from us.'

Fiction is quite different from the previous two albums. For starters it sounds as though something has been resolved, lifting the darkness of SNM. But it also stands Janus-faced, looking backwards to SNM and forwards to Land, their fourth and first post-Polydor album. The first song, After the Rain, clears the air immediately (i.e. rain is a symbol of depression). There are musical residues remaining from SNM and a new version of an earlier song, Ju Ju Money, from the WfaM period. Stephen Fellows comments, 'Looking back I think it's only fair to say that it's a pretty mixed album. We were touring quite a bit after SNM and there wasn't as much time to write as I would have liked. I had the idea that the album was a necessary fiction. I've never enjoyed written fiction that much because, as we know, life doesn't have a plot or a narrator and it rarely makes sense. I was kind of signalling that it was "made up", as opposed to the peddling of the grim reality which we'd been accused of.' This is certainly the case with the song Zinger which includes the line, 'She took a drink from the radio.' This came from a bet Fellows had taken with a friend saying it was possible to make a song from anything. Clearly then, Fiction is a lighter album altogether.

The Minor 3rd from WfaM and SNM, continues to exert an influence. For example, it has been subsumed into the overall harmonic framework of Now I Know, as well as being present in the foreground thematicism. Yet, in the main, the abiding melancholy of SNM is now distanced. The keyboards are also more foregrounded, as opposed to the ambient role they took in SNM. Melodically, the phrase structures are longer as in After the Rain which is now in D minor Dorian (Ex. 68). The rhythmic structure of the melody line has also been freed-up by crotchet triplets.

Pictures is completely memorable and is also transitional. Beyond its E minor modal centre there's a catchy hook-line (Ex. 69). In general, the melodies are beginning to look beyond the new-wave towards mid-1980s pop. The single, It's History, also from this period is one of The Comsats' most original and memorable songs which really should have been a huge hit. Fellows has recently observed 'I like longer melodies or phrases these days. A lot of the older, shorter phrases were an attempt to come up with catchy bits. I sort of let them go where they want now.' The arrangements suggest a half-way house between the previously sparse textures of SNM and the fuller sonic landscapes of their subsequent album, Land.

Ex. 68

When a sky ful of tears_ is threat-ning to fall__

Ex. 69

Torn out al the pa - ges one by one, Put them in the fire____

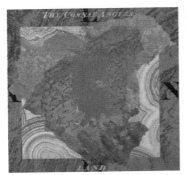

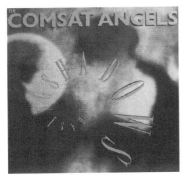

6. Land and beyond

Land and 7 Day Weekend

The mid-period Comsat Angels began when their contract with Polydor wasn't renewed. The band signed for Jive Records. On their first release for the label, Land (1983), the melodies are longer-spanned, opening-out even further than on Fiction. Clearly, a new direction had come into being and the band was being groomed for the mass audience.

The songs Alicia and A World Away demonstrate this new-found freedom. The guitar timbre is also more in keeping with the mid-1980s. The bass and drums in A World Away are, indeed, a world a world away from the rhythmic interest found on WfaM and SNM. Rhythmically, as well as in terms of the vocal phrasing everything is more four-square. The keyboards, centred on the Roland Juno-6, are foregrounded and include many punctuated rhythmic stabs. There's something approaching the Human League's late style, particularly on Mister Memory and I'm Falling from the follow-up 7 Day Weekend where Fellows sounds uncannily like Phil Oakey together with harmony vocals – an unusual approach for the Comsats. The main difference is that the Comsats' songs are minor mode-centred and the arrangements more original, as they continue to offer their own language but in a new mainstream pop context with the album clearly aimed at the commercial market. The reduced arrangements of SNM have also passed in favour of fuller, more direct textures.

The paradox is that the Comsat Angels of Land, and its follow-up 7 Day Weekend – essentially a collection of singles – don't sound like another of the glitzy stylised '80s pop bands. Dealing in a more serious sensibility, and using a high degree of metaphor, for example in Island Heart, this music is far different from that heard in the marketplace and far in advance of mainstream pop. This is not to say that Land and 7 Day Weekend are bad. That is the point. The production, writing and arrangements are of a high quality and there is the sense that what they had done earlier might bear fruit commercially with Land. The issue here is that they seem to have lost their individuality. It's actually still present but concealed behind the emerging pop persona. The earlier singles, such as Do the Empty House and It's History, with its counterpointed verse and chorus material in the final refrain, are distinctive. The material on these mid-period albums is much less so. For example, the made-over Independence Day, re-released as a single includes the rather clichéd dotted crotchet, quaver, crotchet rhythm avoided on the original version. Unlike the banal melodic structures and synthesizer-driven muzak of the Human League's Dare, Stephen Fellows's writing retains the melancholic imprint of his earlier output. Songs like 7 Day Weekend's Believe It, Forever Young and You Move Me are wonderfully crafted. And perhaps this is also the point: inspiration and craft are often quite different avenues of creativity. There's also the case of repeating one's clichés which, in a sense is a case in point on both albums.

The paradox might be that if the Comsats hadn't pursued this path then Fellows's gift for melodic pop might never have been heard. This, if nothing else, was an important stage in his and the band's musical development, whether die-hard fans liked it or not – and many didn't. Their fans were slow to relinquish post-punk subcultural identities and stylistic orientations. (The story of this period of the band is well documented in the sleeve-notes of The Comsat Angels – 7 Day Weekend [Special Edition – Connoisseur VSOP CD 330]).

Chasing Shadows

In 1986 the Comsat Angels were 'rescued' by Robert Palmer from their contract with Jive. It was Palmer, a huge fan of the band, who managed to secure a record deal for them with Island Records. It also turned out that Island label boss, Chris Blackwell also loved the band. As a result they recorded and released their sixth album, Chasing Shadows which was co-produced by Palmer. He also shared the vocals on You'll Never Know. Stephen Fellows subsequently went on to write with Palmer for his album, Don't Explain.

There is something very unusual about Chasing Shadows. Although it is a long way removed from the Jive period it's as though the band are being powered in a direction which isn't quite their own. In other words, it sounds as if the band still isn't being quite true to its own identity. The dark sleeve conveys what is in the music; as if something is in gestation which, on this album, isn't quite brought to birth. Perhaps, unconsciously the band is coming to terms with the 'shadow' of chasing success (their collective shadow?) as the chorus of the title song might suggest. Robert Palmer's influence is paramount throughout, and in places brings to mind the dynamic and rhythmic directness of the Power Station (Palmer, Duran Duran's John and Andy Taylor and Chic's Tony Thompson). More than anywhere else, Chasing Shadows also foregrounds Andy Peake's formidable pianistic skills.

1) The Thought that Counts
This opener is in D major and made from one main component: D – C/D chords. Here, there's also the Stephen Fellows fingerprint of counterpointing important thematic strands in the coda as in the single It's History. Fellows's verse melody outlines a 4th ([C]-D-A) and the memorable chorus extends the 4th downwards (G-F#-E-D) to low D filling in the complete octave (D-D) from verse to chorus.

2) The Cutting Edge
The stand-out track is undoubtedly The Cutting Edge with its walking bass line, improvisatory piano fills and Stephen Fellows's penchant for exquisite, memorable melody. In C# minor, pivot

chords of A-B-C# minor move over the predominantly C# minor walking bass of C#-E-G#-B. As a result of the Island deal, Chris Blackwell financed the band's own studio in Sheffield called Axis. Stephen Fellows remembers, 'I like Cutting Edge and Carried Away and Lost Continent is OK. I wish we'd taken a bit more time over the writing but we were just excited at having done a deal with a dream label. We should have learned by that point. Mick and I were talking recently and we agreed that the bit we enjoyed most was working on the new songs.'

3) Under the Influence
In G# minor, it is a tritone away from the opening The Thought that Counts. The interest in harmonic movement by tritones (Augmented 4th/Diminished 5th) begins in this context except there isn't movement by tritones within individual songs. The influence of Robert Palmer is particularly felt here.

4) Carried Away
This is like a quieter, more passive version of the previous song.

5) You'll Never Know
In D, the song is again Robert Palmer-like with its high-ranged vocal. Palmer also shares the vocals by singing in the middle section.

6) Lost Continent
In A, this includes tribal drumming together with an archetypal 1980s texture of muted guitar arpeggios and long sustained keyboards. There is a strong chorus melody and the texture is spacious.

7) Flying Dreams
Again in A, the song begins with solo piano followed by a loud octave guitar quaver and quaver rest rhythm (4/4: q/q/qr/q/q/qr/q/q| qr/q/q/qr/q/q/qr) reminiscent of Robert Fripp's introduction to King Crimson's Fracture (1973). The song is, however, harmonically static.

8) Pray for Rain
This is essentially a song for voice and piano which highlights Andy Peake's piano skills.

The album structure is strong but is harmonically more static as compared with their previous work and texturally less interesting. There is something underlying this album that doesn't quite add up. It's as though the band were hoping to return to their pre-Jive atmospheres but, at the same time, are searching for something new. In this sense, Chasing Shadows and their stint with Island Records are transitional.

After saying all this, I have to say I find Chasing Shadows strangely compelling. Besides its memorable songs, excellent performance and production it's the grey, shadowiness of it all - particularly the sleeve-art - signifying a kind of dark optimism: as though the band have found a footing and are now looking forward to a productive time of engagement with a potential future with Island Records, but with a kind of doubt lurking at the back of it all - pessimism, even - suggested in some of Fellows's lyrics. For example, there's inflation ('Flying Dreams'); both depression and catharsis are symbolised by the rain in 'Pray for Rain'; the shadow in 'The Thought that Counts'. This adds up to an ever-shifting symbolic experience as opposed to the merely semiotic. It's as though something's been found but, at the same time balanced by an ever-present sense of loss. It's this kind of compensatory side on Comsat Angels records which provides a listener with an experience of wholeness. With its mainly minor modes and dark sleeve-art, Chasing Shadows encapsulates Stephen Fellows's statement 'ecstatic melancholy' for describing the band's oeuvre. In a sense the album is something of a paradox but, in Jungian terms, there is always gold to be had from the shadow.

Listening to Chasing Shadows on vinyl is a different experience from the CD version. The structure is sharply delineated with the eight songs being divided exactly as 4x4 on each side, respectively. You'll Never Know, as the first song on side two, is evenly balanced with side one's opener, The Thought That Counts. Both are unified by D. There is a shift upwards to the Dominant (A) for Lost Continent and Flying Dreams, followed by the interrupted cadential movement to B major for the final song, Pray for Rain. Interestingly, the song (and the album as a whole) closes on G# minor: this is not only the relative minor to B major, but a tritone distant from the album's D centre. In a sense, the album connects with Sleep No More, but is more direct and, perhaps, the resolution to the former.

Fire on the Moon

Following Chasing Shadows the Comsat Angels were threatened with legal action by the Comsat Communication Company from the USA for using the Comsat brand name. They had already been forced to use the name The CS Angels for US releases. For the follow-up to Chasing Shadows the band changed their name to the Dream Command releasing their seventh album, Fire on the Moon in 1990.

Again, this record sounds like a stab at the pop market and, like King Crimson's Beat, there's something about it which I feel doesn't quite work. Perhaps it's too self-consciously aimed at the commercial market. The music sounds somehow contrived; made as opposed to inspired. As a result their contract with Island Records came to an end. Stephen Fellows remembers: 'Fire on the Moon was the real point of transition. Everything about it was such a disaster that I was determined, whatever happened, not to do a record like that anymore. No more music would be made to fit an "idea" of what we should be doing, i.e. commercial rock/pop music that would get on US radio. It was Kev pushing this idea mostly but the rest of us went along with it. There didn't seem any point doing anymore if it wasn't "real" - that's how I saw it anyway. I really had to pretty much 'drive' MME myself to get it finished - at one point there was only me and Andy left in the band, even so, I knew it was good and hoped that it would pull everyone together again.' The exceptions are Ice Sculpture with its G/D - A/E - slap bass part and a texture which owes something to King Crimson's The Sheltering Sky from Discipline. Venus Hunter also points forward to My Mind's Eye. The double-CD, To Before, includes demos of this period taken from the band's own archives. Somehow, these sound more in keeping with the Comsats' own identity without record company interference.

Fire on the Moon also came close to the end of 1980s when rock music was preparing for a revolution with the anticipation of the compact-disc and digital technology, alongside the rediscovery of the previous generation's music. That the final song on Fire on the Moon is called Mercury may be significant: not only was Mercury messenger of the gods but, more importantly, was the great god of the alchemists; it was he who brought transformation and change during the alchemical opus. And it is the most fertile period of the Comsats' career that lay just around the corner.

Photo © Simon Robinson / www.easyontheeye.net

7. My Mind's Eye

The return to authentic Comsat Angels' form was signalled by the two albums released on RPM/Thunderbird in 1992 and 1995, respectively: My Mind's Eye and The Glamour.

Both were re-released in CD format in 2007 by Renascent with subtle track re-orderings. It strikes me that the band ceased trying to be commercially successful instead returning to what they were best at: tasteful, imaginative and meaningful indie music. The first thing that strikes a listener in My Mind's Eye is the more guitar-based and up-front, regular rhythmic drum patterning. The drums and bass are rhythmically more regular and the tribal rhythmic impetus, notable in the 1980s, has more or less vanished. Certainly, this has much to do with the zeitgeist. At the time the Brit Pop scene had taken hold of the nation with the media-hyped war of words between Oasis and Blur. U2 had also recently released Achtung Baby and the Stone Roses were being promoted as the vanguard of a neo-psychedelic Manchester scene. Stephen Fellows has said that 'My Mind's Eye is my favourite Comsat Angels album.'

The album concentrates on inner states: Eastern spirituality, science fiction, psychedelia but without recourse to meta-narratives or the 'big' questions. The sleeve-notes credit Jimi Hendrix, Arvo Part (both huge influences on Stephen Fellows) and also American agnostic mystic Robert Anton Wilson (author of The Illuminatus Trilogy [1975] which documents the counter-culture, the occult, conspiracy theories and so on) and Harold Weisberg, one of the leading experts on the assassination of John F. Kennedy. There is also a collage designed by Fellows of planets, a US high-level reconnaissance plane, Krishna, JFK, Lee Harvey Oswald, a poster of The Illuminatus and, central to it a photo of the band on a spiral-staircase. These provide visual clues to the album's contents. MME, as the title suggests, is the world of the imaginary conveyed in the entire concept although this is a world away from prog rock.

There is altogether something as musically and lyrically infectious as the Beatles' Revolver or Jimi Hendrix's Axis: Bold as Love. Spacious ambient textures, strong melodies, meaningful harmonic content, delineated overdriven and clean guitars, driving bass and drums give MME a distinctive flavour somehow new and old at the same time and certainly leaning towards American cultural signifiers conveyed in some of the songs. In a sense, it is a musical counterpart to Robert Anton Wilson's literary work. Andy Peake's wide-ranging keyboard atmospheres/ambience provides an unparalleled and original perspective on orchestration connecting MME with SNM. Somehow, the music is inward looking and it is, perhaps, this reliance on 'questing' that place the Comsats outside the contemporary; perhaps close to the late '60s and early '70s countercultural concerns than the music of mass appeal surrounding it. Maybe this is the reason for their neglect by the wider listening public intent on quick fixes rather than considered and intelligent musico-philosophical experience.

1) Driving
The big, double-tracked guitar texture of Driving was a massive shock to Comsat Angels' fans on its release. This powerful opener begins with a bright D major chord followed by B/E/B guitar chords underpinned by C# in the bass and then G. The tritone (Augmented 4th/Diminished 5th), so important on MME and The Glamour, is first heard here in this context (i.e. C#-G). The chorus also includes the tritone in the context of A-E/G#-D-E/G#

and then, again, D-Ab-G. On first hearing, it seems that the Minor 3rds, so prevalent on early Comsats music, have been replaced with a new musical vocabulary. The keyboards glue the texture together with sustained chords.

2) Always Near
This has a strong, memorable melody with the opening clean guitar instrumental hook close to some of their earlier work (B [3rd string to open B second string] – A-D-E-F#). However, the song is more direct rhythmically with an acoustic guitar accompaniment and the fingerprint electric guitar doubling the voice in the chorus section. Andy Peake's keyboards subtly orchestrate and colour the spaces in the texture by outlining the harmonics of guitar chords. There is also a Hendrix-like clean solo in the middle which, again, outlines the melody.

3) Beautiful Monster
This opens with clean guitar power-chords on the 3rd and 4th strings over an open A on frets 7 – 4 – 3 – 10. The guitar includes lots of chords minus the 3rd.

4) Shiva Descending
Shiva Descending is probably the finest moment on the album, with its martial snare-drum and opening rising half-tone B-C-B-A guitar hookline foregrounding the semitone ascent which was to become important on The Glamour. The keyboards (strings and organ) create a shimmering orchestration. Fellows has said that 'Hinduism – I did read a bit about it. I studied Rajah Yoga with the Bramah Kumaris.' The clean guitar is minimally applied to the beginning of bars and there's always great musical economy. From 1:59ff the chords Am/C-B/-Em7-D-C outlines a series of parallel first inversions. The keyboards in verse three heighten the words 'Lately I find myself thinking in terms of the kingdom/And all I can hear at this time is the sound of the drum.' Mik Glaisher's drum ostinato is also important to the lyrics. Fellows reiterates, 'I don't regard the lyrics as autobiographical, but I may be wrong.' (See appendix for a transcription of the song).

5) My Mind's Eye
The title song has a high-powered pre-Foo Fighters-like power-chorded texture of Bm-G9 (fret 10)-E9 (fret 7)-G9 (fret 10). In the verses the guitar again doubles the falling vocal line (C#-B-A-G-

F#) and in the coda wah-wah guitar is introduced. The lyrics provide a further insight into the album's content:

Verse 1

Had a vista vision
Future space and time
We are on a mission
Burn it up
Speed of light
To the end
Of the sky
And I watch as the silver ships climb
In my mind's eye.

Verse 2

Action at a distance
Mountains of the moon
Reason for existence
Turn it up
Power drive
Everything
Is alive
Dreamed I saw the vermillion sunrise
In my mind's eye.

This is a Romantic vision close to Coleridge and, certainly the visionary poetry of William Blake. It is also reminiscent of countercultural concerns of the mid-1960s.

6) I Come from the Sun
This song looks back to Dark Parade on SNM and has an affinity with Pink Floyd's Set the Controls for the Heart of the Sun. The bass outlines a rising half-tone (E-F) and the vocal melody (A-B-A-B-C-B) refers not only to the semitone but also refers back to the guitar hookline of Shiva Descending. It points forward to the Eastern references in such songs as Psychedelic Dungeon and Oblivion (D-C-Eb-D) and Valley of the Nile on The Glamour.

7) Field of Tall Flowers
The song has a distinct summer-feel and is, essentially, an

acoustic guitar-based song. Instantly memorable, the melody outlines the modal Minor 3rd which is a Stephen Fellows fingerprint: C#-E-D#-C#-B-C#. The chorus has electric guitar arpeggiated chords of C# minor – B/D# - C#/E with spoken words over the middle section.

8) Route 666
This song deals with the avoidance of truth and reinforces the C-F# tritone.

9) Mystery Plane
A strange American sci-fi feel occupies this song with its Minor 3rd bass A-C-D-G-A riff, the snare shuffle and the strangeness of the keyboard strings. In a way, it is close to the music of '60s instrumental band, The Tornados. The guitar is delay-drenched doubling the voice in 6ths. The lyrics continue the inscapes at the centre of the album:

Verse 1

I'm out of my depth
It's out of my hands
Mystery plane
I don't understand
Don't mention the lies
The things that you said
Mystery plane
I'm back here again.

Chorus

And still I wonder
And I scratch my head
Maybe there's a meaning
I've not found it yet.

Verse 2

Find what you seek
Seek what you find
Mystery plane
It's all in your mind

Do anything

Can't trust how you feel

Mystery plane
Nothing is real.

Chorus

Maybe there's a reason
For the way it goes
Maybe there's a reason
But you'll never know.

10) And All the Stars

Again, this has a '60s American sci-fi feel heightened by the tremolo keyboards (a saxophone sample on the Emax). Harmonically, the song is made from three chords: E-E/G#-D with the chorus melody outlining an E major chord: E-G#-E-E-B-G#-E-(F#). The guitar chords at the beginning of each bar are 'clipped' cleanly, reminiscent of Peter Green and the keyboards sustain E. The central guitar solo is just a sprinkling of pitches with, mainly, left-hand clean Stratocaster guitar glissandi and bends. It wells-up at the end underpinned by Glaisher's exact drumming. The keyboards, on their own, signify the changeover of styles from the new-wave of the 1980s to the neo-psychedelia of the early '90s. Here there is a fusion - a conjunction of all the Comsats had been striving for up to this time.

Photo © Simon Robinson / www.easyontheeye.net

8. The Glamour

The Glamour was originally released by RPM/Thunderbird in 1995 and re-released by Renascent as a double album in 2007. The Renascent release is different from the original. The Glamour continues the vibrancy of My Mind's Eye. This is the first album without bass player Kevin Bacon and, as a result, the band expanded to a five-piece with the addition of Terry Todd on bass and Simon Anderson on second guitar.

The original track-listing on the 1995 release is:

1) Psychedelic Dungeon
2) The Glamour
3) Audrey in Denim
4) Oblivion
5) Web of Sound
6) Breaker
7) SS100X
8) Sailor
9) Demon Lover
10) Pacific Ocean Blues
11) Anjelica

12) Valley of the Nile
13) Spaced

The double-album re-release is:

CD 1
1) I Hear A New World
2) Goddess
3) Anjelica
4) Valley of the Nile
5) Sailor
6) Pacific Ocean Blues
7) Oblivion
8) The Naila Game
9) Audrey in Denim
10) Demon Lover

CD 2
1) Psychedelic Dungeon
2) SS100X
3) The Glamour
4) Breaker
5) Evanescent
6) Hyperprism 1
7) Spaced
8) Web of Sound
9) A Song called Dave
10) Slayer of the Real

Stephen Fellows notes on the Renascent CD cover that, 'We were prevented by deadlines from finishing all the music we were recording – this is much closer to how it should have been. We've added eight previously unreleased recordings, including five previously unreleased songs. It's just about everything the five-piece recorded.' The unreleased material fits the scheme of the original admirably. Fellows also says, 'In case it's not apparent the title is ironic!' Like the very best of the Comsat Angels, The Glamour reflects the zeitgeist and it does so in the present context with its neo-psychedelic atmospheres and song structures, wah-wah laden textures, Phrygian and Locrian semitonal shifts along with some acoustic guitar textures. It's possible to hear the influence of mid-period Beatles, Hendrix and

Syd Barrett-era Pink Floyd particularly in the harmonic context.
Also, there is, in places an allusion to Can-like Krautrock styles
for example in the looped mantra-like lines of Psychedelic
Dungeon. At the time, the scene was dominated by the likes of
Oasis with Wonderwall blasting across the airwaves, the Beatles-
like structures of Lenny Kravitz, the Smashing Pumpkins, the
Pixies and so on. David Sylvian and Robert Fripp had also had a
successful album, The First Day – with its psychedelic/Hendrix-
like flavouring – and the double-trio, mid-90s King Crimson
released Thrak in the same year.

I will discuss The Glamour in the context of the original 1995
release although, in many ways, I prefer the more recent double-
album which paradoxically improves yet, at the same time, takes
something away from the original's stark and direct sonic
approach. Although the album sounds a thousand miles away
from SNM it is, in fact, identifiably Comsat Angels and not just
through Fellows's distinctive voice: the ambient Comsat
ambient/atmospherics fingerprint is a thread which binds all
their output together. The Glamour, as with the very best of the
Comsats output, allows an audient to penetrate a personal, muse-
driven sound-world which is at once melancholic and laden with
minor keys. There is a certain gravity present in this music which
is not apparent in the work of their close contemporaries such as
Oasis.

1) Psychedelic Dungeon
This is in A minor beginning with a kind of looped mantra (Ex.
70) which is doubled with distorted electric guitar. The lyrics deal
with altered states:

'I'm studying the ceiling
Can't tear myself away
I'm busy doing nothing
And it's going to take all day.
Contemplating space and time
Her body and the fate of Brian Jones
Wondering about the world outside etc.'

The chords are more direct and powerful with the presence of two
guitars in the band and essentially: (Verses) Am; (Choruses) Em-
G-Em-G/C-D 5ths.

2) The Glamour

The title song is made from interlocking tritone chords: C#-G-E-Bb making a diminished quartal chord. It races along with its wah-wah saturated texture and Hendrix-like guitar bends all heightening the ironic lyrics. This song is another aspect of the glamour concept at the root of the album.

3) Audrey in Denim

Steve Fellows describes the genesis of the song and also Anjelica: 'The protagonists are both real. The latter is an actress; the former an ex-colleague of my wife's who turned up at a works do wearing an all-denim ensemble that was considered at least twenty five years too young for her. A friend said "Hmmm, Audrey in denim." I thought it was a good metaphor for being in a band and having to trot it all out again when you feel you're too old and embarrassed. I was fairly sure that it was going to be our last album. Rather than ironic, it was intended to be sarcastic, musically, in places. The first version of the album was only released like that because of deadlines. If we'd have had the time and the support it would have more closely resembled the newer version.' The song has a distinct swagger to it, and is something which might have influenced fellow Sheffield musician, and former Longpigs guitarist Richard Hawley. The D-F-Bb-A opening also underpins the chorus. The unison quaver guitar phrases which connect verses to chorus (D-E-F-G-A-Bb-C-C#) owe something to the coda of Hendrix's Hey Joe and, here, are equally as powerful. The clean, vibrato-less Farfisa timbre of the verses is also notable for its banality. In this context, the Comsats become like a belated club band to drive home the metaphorical concept of the song.

4) Oblivion

The song is effects-laden and emphasise the half-tone motivic shifts in the song: D-C-Db. The acoustic guitar part is notable with its A-Bb inner-part movement within a D 5ths chord also reinforcing the Phrygian shift which is a thread throughout the album. The electric piano part mixes with the guitar and at 2:16 provides a memorable instrumental hook (Ex. 71). As in SNM, the keyboards add to the strangeness at the back of the album.

5) Web of Sound
This is a powerful song with its D-Bm power-chord introduction playing over a root D in the bass. The two guitars don't play identically: instead, the second guitar plays powerful D chords over the first guitar's Bm.

6) Breaker
The influence of Jimi Hendrix and the Beatles is felt here in the opening clean electric guitar (Ex. 72), over the sound of ambient wave-like noise. It develops with suspended E, becoming E major and transforming to E minor (Ex. 73).

7) SS 100X
The verse chords are memorable for their 1960s feel: E-C-F#m-F and the tritone (C-F#) which connects much of the album. Again, the Comsat Angels owe more to the 1960s than the 1970s connecting their earlier work with this later offering. SS 100X is about denial and illusion: what really happened at John F. Kennedy's assassination. This is part of the 'concept' of The Glamour: JFK was part of the '60s thus decoding the reality of illusion. Fellows sheds light on some of the lyrics: ' "A thousand pieces in the breeze" refers to Bobby Kennedy's threat (promise) to break the CIA into a thousand pieces and scatter them to the winds; "1, 2, 3" was the official number of shots; "Take care the company you keep" those who work for the CIA refer to it as The Company; "4, 5, 6" is the number of alleged further shots, although some conspiracy freaks reckon that it was as many as eleven.' The rhythm guitar-driven harmonic basis (Em-C-F#-F and its pivot-pitch modulation) makes it one of the strongest songs on The Glamour.

8) Sailor
This is essentially a vocal over a repeated electric guitar chordal mantra (Ex. 74). The chords are Em7-C#m7-Am7-Em7.

9) Demon Lover
Tritones are again emphasised (E-G-C#) in this direct and powerful song.

10) Pacific Ocean Blues
Here there are pivot-note shifts between chords (Am-Ab-Bb). The Am and Ab chords are connected by C natural and included in the

guitar arpeggios which introduce each verse (Ex. 75). The power-chords of the verses are again connected through tritones: C-Bb-C-Bb-C-Bb-C-Db-C-Bb/E-D-E-D-E-D-E-F-E-D. The upward semitone shift is also emphasised (C-Db/E-F). The sea, both in this and in Sailor, is a symbol par excellence of the collective unconscious. Beyond this, the song is direct and melodically memorable.

11) Anjelica
Stephen Fellows has previously mentioned the protagonist of the song. A harmonic glissando begins leading to loud D-F-G-Bb chords – a cliché in some musical circles – with a memorable instrumental hook of D-E-F-E-D-E-F-E-D between the verses. The double quaver snare drum attacks on every third phrase of the chorus make this song thoroughly memorable.

12) Valley of the Nile
This song is both archetypal and muse-driven, inspired by a poster Fellows saw of the Egyptian pyramids. It is underpinned by acoustic guitar A 5th chords where the E descends to Eb, again making the tritone connection easy to hear and 'Egyptian' in its overall sound (Ex. 76). The mellotron-like keyboards play material from a Lydian scale beginning on A (Ex. 77). The verses are essentially drone-like on A with the bass sometimes playing an F# (part of the Lydian aggregate), while the choruses are underpinned by D-F#-A-B-C#-E-D#-D-C#. Fellows plays a Robert Fripp-like solo from 2:26ff. Valley of the Nile is one of the most memorable of the songs on The Glamour.

13) Spaced
Spaced completes the album with its delay-saturated vocals and pivot-note shifting between chords of A and F majors. One is immediately reminded of both late Syd Barrett and Atom Heart Mother-era Pink Floyd.

Notable on the double album re-release of The Glamour is 'Goddess'. It uses what Fellows has called geometry. He writes in the sleeve-notes to From Beyond – A Compilation 1987 – 1995 'Goddess hopefully illustrates the power of geometry. It's got more of those chords that I mentioned earlier, but with a kind of baroque/surf vibe in the changes.' I Hear a New World also became a favourite 'live' number, pointing-up the apparent difference between the old and new versions of the band which are, paradoxically, the same but always different.

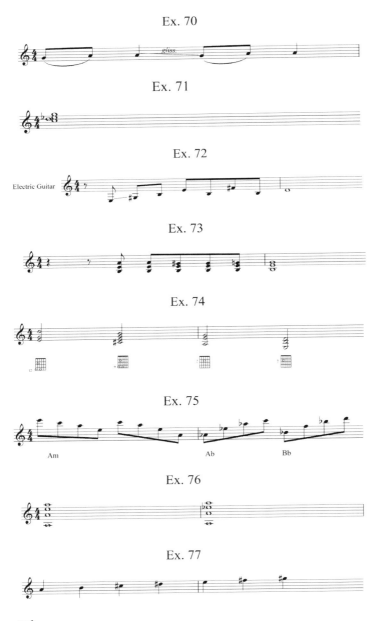

9. Conclusion

I have a lot of albums: both CDs and vinyl. I'm currently thinking of selling the whole lot except for a couple of boxes full. These include records by King Crimson, Robert Fripp, McDonald and Giles, Nick Drake, T2, Cross and Ross, the Beatles, Judee Sill, John Tavener, John Foxx and the Comsat Angels. For me, these albums are worth keeping because the music has retained its power and integrity throughout the years. It's held up incredibly well. Beyond that, they provide the soundtracks to particular periods of the generations in which they were conceived.

It usually takes me a couple of listens through to an album to identify the music's power; if it has a chance of holding up in the years to come. Some albums I buy through media hype (silly, I know) and because I'm a dedicated follower of fashion. We all like to buy fashionable things. But, the older I become the sillier it all seems. It may sound fatalistic but it strikes me as we bring nothing into this world we won't be taking anything out with us. What's the point of holding onto things which aren't worth holding onto? Plus, why should I be drawn into corporate thinking? The best music was always a reaction to that. Perhaps that's what I identify in the bands and musicians I've listed above? These musicians made music of lasting power. They may be not be known by the mass audience but – and this may sound a really elitist statement – what do they care?

The music of the Comsat Angels has been a good friend over the years. It's something I often return to. Their music is enduring. It has an integrity that I don't hear in much other music. This present writing has identified some of those things which have intrigued me about the band: the brilliance of WfaM; the darkness of SNM; the melodic beauty of Fiction; the directness and power of My Mind's Eye; the metaphorical significance of The Glamour. Somehow there seems to be a wholeness in the music and that's maybe what I sense when listening to real, organic music as opposed to stylised, synthetic and 'made' product. What I hear in the Comsat Angels may come down to two points: excellent musicianship; original, creative thought; considered production values.

I had the good fortune to work with Stephen Fellows on several of my Otherworld projects – my 'shadow' alt rock recording ensemble which comes into being as and when the music presents itself. In fact, Steve coined the title, Otherworld. He's played and sung on Bells of Heaven, Hyde, My Red Book and a further one in progress at this moment. It's become clear to me that in the process of working with him there's a distinct and real musical mind at work and it's this mind that helped steer the Comsat Angels through the 1980s and '90s. Clearly, he's a musician in the very real sense of the word. For me, Steve is a musical hero. Each member of the Comsats – probably, as in any band – has a particular function besides their vocal or instrumental contribution. However, the load is shared in a whole and complete way in the band: Stephen Fellows – songwriter and conceptualist; Andy Peake – orchestrator and soundscaper; Kevin Bacon – sonic organiser/producer; Mick Glaisher – rhythmic deconstructionist; Terry Todd - ace bassist.

The more I explored, unravelled and analysed the more I discovered that perhaps the music of the Comsats both is and isn't the soundtrack of the period(s) in which they worked. Superficially, they make pertinent outer observations (Dark Parade) but, simultaneously, observe inwardly (I Come from the Sun). In other words, the work tends towards introspection. Songs, such as the latter, I have described as 'inscapes' or, at least the band delve into quasi-countercultural concerns mostly obscured from the mass audience.

In this way, I do and don't find it surprising that commercial success evaded the band. It's clear when listening to their music that it presents a different way of doing things. I saw the reformed Comsat Angels in Sheffield on 26th April, 2009 and in Manchester on 23rd October, 2009. The sense I had at both concerts was that here was a band who had reached cult proportions of an act such as the Velvet Underground. Nearly a thousand people attended the Sheffield show, some from as far away as Canada. To my ears the music sounded enduring. But, clearly it was music of an indie type and perhaps this is why the Comsat Angels, as a mid-'80s pop band, failed to register. In my honest opinion, I think the music is too considered, too complex and just too damn good to be wasted on the mediocre commercial pop market. As in the early 1970s where mass pop music was centred on the likes of Slade and Mud, the 1980s mass market was identified by Spandau Ballet, ABC and so on. The underground/Indie scene was populated by the likes of Joy Division, The Sound, Music for Pleasure, Cabaret Voltaire etc with the distinction being made between bands signed to major labels or independents such as Factory. The Comsats were signed to Polydor which, due to the strength of their music, didn't actually alienate them as had been the case with early Ultravox, for example, signed to Island.

The best are rarely known in their own lifetimes, which is probably the biggest crime against humanity in the history of crime. But, nevertheless, it's a truism. The best are often overlooked because they stand apart from the crowd. This is individuation as against mass-mindedness; the goats against the sheep. It seems to me that this is the case with the Comsat Angels. Their achievement is in the process of becoming known and, as far as I'm concerned, they stand head and shoulders above their close contemporaries. They're often referred to in the music press and bands cite them as influential. I hope this guide to their music brings their output to the attention of more people: it, and they, demand to be known.

10. Discography

Albums

Waiting For A Miracle
1980, Polydor
(Re-released, Renascent 2006)

Sleep No More
1981, Polydor
(Re-released, Renascent 2006)

Fiction
1982, Polydor
(Re-released, Renascent 2006)

Land
1983 - 2001, Jive Connoisseur

7 Day Weekend
1985 - 2001, Jive Connoisseur

Chasing Shadows
1986, Island

Fire On The Moon
1990, Island

My Mind's Eye
1992, RPM / Thunderbird
(Re-released, Renascent 2007)

The Glamour
1995, RPM / Thunderbird
(Re-released, Renascent 2006)

Unravelled
Dutch radio sessions
1993/94, RPM, 1994

From Beyond - a Comsat Angels Compilation
2000, Cherry Red

Time considered as a helix of semi-precious stones
The BBC sessions 1974 - 1984
2006, Renascent

To Before
2007, Renascent

Singles

Red Planet EP
1979, Junta Records

Total War EP
1980, Polydor

Independence Day
1980, Polydor

Eye Of The Lens
1981, Polydor

(Do The) Empty House
1981, Polydor

It's History
May 1982, Polydor

After The Rain
1982, Polydor

Will You Stay Tonight?
1983, Jive

Island Heart
1983, Jive

Independence Day (re-recording)
1984, Jive

You Move Me
1984, Jive

Day One
1984, Jive

I'm Falling
1985, Jive

Forever Young
1985, Jive

The Cutting Edge
1986, Island

Celestine
1990, Island

Driving
1992, RPM Thunderbird

Shiva Descending
1993, Crisis Records

Field Of Tall Flowers
1993, RPM Thunderbird

The Cutting Edge
1994, Crisis Records

11. Comsat Angels - gig list

1977
07.09.77 Sheffield Broadfield Pub (as Radio Earth)

1978
18.11.78 Newcastle University (as Radio Earth)

1979
04.04.79 Lincoln Art College , England
25.06.79 Doncaster Sports Club, England
07.07.79 Sheffield Broadfield Hotel, England
29.07.79 Amsterdam Melkweg, Holland
09.09.79 Amstelveen De Bajes, Holland
??.09.79 Hilversum Tagrijn, Holland
??.09.79 Vlissingen De Piek, Holland
23.09.79 Amsterdam Melkveg, Holland
14.11.79 Sheffield Broadfield Hotel, England

1980
18.03.80 Sheffield George IV, The Blitz, England
??.06.80 Sheffield University Platform 1, England
04.09.80 Amsterdam Melkveg, Holland
05.09.80 Haarlem Dagblad, Holland
??.09.80 Hilversum Tagrijn, Holland
16.09.80 Rotterdam, Holland

??.09.80 Vlissingen De Piek, Holland
20.09.80 London Clapham 101 Club, England
21.09.80 London Herne Hill Half Moon, England
22.09.80 London Islington Hope And Anchor, England
24.09.80 London Canning Town Bridge House, England
05.10.80 London Lyceum, England
11.10.80 Oxford New Theatre, England
12.10.80 Birmingham Odeon, England
13.10.80 Manchester Apollo, England
15.10.80 London Marquee, England
16.10.80 London Hammersmith Odeon, England
18.10.80 Southampton Gaumont, England
25.10.80 Cardiff University, Wales
26.10.80 Bristol Colston Hall, England
27.10.80 Birmingham Odeon, England
28.10.80 Glasgow Apollo, Scotland
29.10.80 Liverpool Rotters, England
30.10.80 Manchester Apollo, England
04.11.80 Leeds Warehouse, England
05.11.80 Coventry Warwick University, England
06.11.80 London Hammersmith Clarendon Hotel, England
07.11.80 Sheffield Polytechnic, England
08.11.80 Edinburgh Nite Club, Scotland
10.11.80 London Fulham Greyhound, England
11.11.80 Nottingham Boat Club, England
12.11.80 Derby Blue Note Club, England
13.11.80 Hull Wellington Club, England
14.11.80 Retford Porterhouse, England
15.11.80 Reading University, England
16.11.80 Brighton Jenkinson's, England
17.11.80 Southend Zero 6, England
18.11.80 London Marquee, England (cancelled) changed to Norwich
Cromwells, England
20.11.80 Manchester Rafters, England
21.11.80 Stoke North Staffs Polytechnic, England
22.11.80 Middlesbrough Rock Garden, England
24.11.80 Bradford University, England changed to Liverpool Brady's,
England
25.11.80 Canterbury Kent University, England
26.11.80 Bristol The Berkeley, England
27.11.80 Newport Baileys, Wales
28.11.80 Bournemouth Town Hall, England
29.11.80 London Fulham Greyhound, England changed to London
Marquee, England
5.12.80 Aston University, Birmingham, England

1981
09.02.81 Sheffield University Bar 2, England

16.02.81 Hammersmith Palais, England
17.02.81 Hammersmith Palais, England
19.02.81 Poole Arts Centre, England
20.02.81 Portsmouth Guildhall, England
22.02.81 Leicester De Montfort Hall, England
23.02.81 Derby Assembly Rooms, England
25.02.81 Leeds University, England
27.02.81 Edinburgh Playhouse, Scotland
01.03.81 Liverpool Royal Court, England
03.03.81 Newcastle City Hall, England
07.04.81 London Sundown, England s
22.04.81 Amsterdam Paradiso, Holland
23.04.81 Groningen Vera, Holland
24.04.81 Eindhoven Effenaar, Holland
25.04.81 Rotterdam Eksit, Holland
26.04.81 Apeldoorn Gigant, Holland
??.??.81 Pink Pop Festival, Geleen/Landgraaf?, Holland
03.05.81 Berlin Kant Kino, Germany
26.06.81 Liverpool Brady's, England
27.06.81 Newcastle University, England
30.06.81 Sheffield Top Rank, England
16.08.81 New Pop Festival, Rotterdam
??.09.81 Groningen Vera, Holland
04.09.81 Amsterdam Paradiso, Holland
05.09.81 Stafford Bingley Hall, England Futurama 3 Festival
18.09.81 Edinburgh Nite Club, Scotland
19.09.81 Aberdeen The Venue, Scotland (changed to Victoria Hotel)
20.09.81 Kirk Levington Country Club, England
22.09.81 Manchester Polytechnic, England
23.09.81 York T.A. Centre, England
24.09.81 Leeds Warehouse, England
25.09.81 Sheffield Polytechnic, England
26.09.81 Birmingham Opposite Lock, England (changed to Cedar Ballroom) - cancelled
27.09.81 Bath Tiffany's, England
??.09.81 Groningen Vera, Holland
01.10.81 Norwich East Anglia University, England
02.10.81 Nottingham Rock City, England
03.10.81 Salford University, England
04.10.81 Glasgow Tiffany's, Scotland
06.10.81 Coventry Warwick University, England
07.10.81 Leicester Polytechnic, England
08.10.81 Sheffield Lyceum, England
09.10.81 Newcastle Mayfair, England
10.10.81 Liverpool Royal Court Theatre, England
12.10.81 Brighton Top Rank, England
13.10.81 Portsmouth Locarno, England

14.10.81 Cardiff Top Rank, Wales
16.10.81 Stoke King's Hall, England
17.10.81 Bracknell Sports Centre, England
18.10.81 Bristol Locarno, England
19.10.81 Birmingham Locarno, England
20.10.81 Leeds Tiffany's, England
21.10.81 Hemel Hempstead Pavilion, England
02.11.81 Bedford Corn Exchange, England
03.11.81 London Dominion Theatre, England
04.11.81 Birmingham Keele University, England
05.11.81 Liverpool Warehouse, England
07.11.81 Belfast Queens University, Northern Ireland
08.11.81 Dublin McGonagles, Eire
11.11.81 Canterbury Kent University, England
??.11.81 Hilversum Tagrijn, Holland
27.11.81 Den Haag,Paard van Troje, Holland
28.11.81 Arnhem Stokvishal, Holland
29.11.81 Hargen Rock Palace, Holland
30.11.81 Berlin Cantkino, Germany
02.12.81 Tubingen University Mensa, Wilhelmstrasse, West Germany
03.12.81 Wiesbaden Wartburg, West Germany
04.12.81 Kassel Treiblens, West Germany
05.12.81 Bochum Zeche, West Germany
06.12.81 Hamburg Markthalle, West Germany
07.12.81 Hanover Rotation, West Germany
08.12.81 Muenster Jovel Cinema, West Germany
09.12.81 Osnabrueck Hydepark, Austria
10.12.81 Dortmund Jara, West Germany
11.12.81 Koutrijk Limelight, Belgium
12.12.81 Brussels Generation 80 TV Show, Belgium
??.12.81 Sheffield, England (free gig for unemployed)

1982
04.06.82 Rotterdam Park Pop Festival, Holland
04.07.82 Den Haag Park Pop Festival, Holland
15.07.82 1st gig Philadelphia Ripley's Music Hall, USA
16.07.82 Washington DC Ontario Theatre, USA
17.7.82 New York The Ritz, USA
18.07.82 Boston Paradise Theatre, USA
19.07.82Montreal Le Pretzel, Canada
20.07.82 Toronto Larry's Hideaway, Ontario, Canada
22.07.82 Ann Arbor Hill Auditorium, Michigan Theatre USA
??.08.82 Reykjavik, Iceland
21.08.82 Wateringen Waterpop Festival, Holland
22.08.82 Groningen Vera Zomermanifestatie, Holland
13.09.82 Liverpool Warehouse, England
14.09.82 Leeds Warehouse, England

15.09.82 London Venue, England 16.10.82 Nottingham Whispers, England
17.10.82 London Lyceum, England
20.10.82 Utrecht Tivoli, Holland
21.10.82 Amsterdam Paradiso, Holland
22.10.82 Den Haag Het Paard Van Troje, Holland
23.10.82 Arnhem Stokvishal, Holland
24.10.82 Hamburg Markthalle, West Germany

1983
27.01.83 London Brixton Ace (?? for Channel 4 TV)
28.03.83 Sheffield Leadmill, England
31.03.83 Rotterdam Arena, Holland + interview on Vara FM
01.04.83 Amsterdam Paradiso, Holland
02.04.83 Noord Scharwoude De Koog, Holland
03.04.83 Vaals Spuugh, Holland
04.04.83 Etten-Leur Pop-Inn Festival, Holland
??.??.83 Pink Pop Festival, Holland
??.??.83 Park Pop Festival, Rotterdam Holland
19.08.83 Eindhoven PSV Stadion, Holland
20.08.83 Uden Nieuwe Pul, Holland
21.08.83 Heiloo Bukpop Festival, Holland
23.08.83 London Venue, England
17.09.83 Futurama 5 Festival, Leeds Queens Hall, England
05.10.83 London Trent Park Middlesex Polytechnic, England
06.10.83 Coventry Polytechnic, England
07.10.83 Kingston Polytechnic, England
08.10.83 Birmingham Tin Can Club, England
10.10.83 Sheffield University, England
11.10.83 Liverpool The System, England
12.10.83 Manchester Adam & Eve, England (BBC Radio 1 In Concert recording)
13.10.83 Leicester University, England
14.10.83 Rayleigh Crocs, England
15.10.83 Canterbury Kent University, England
16.10.83 Manchester University Main Debating Hall, England
19.10.83 Vlaardingen Junushof, Holland
20.10.83 Amsterdam Paradiso, Holland
21.10.83 Utrecht Tivoli, Holland
22.10.83 Rotterdam Arena, Holland
23.10.83 Zwolle Jsselhal, Holland
24.10.83 Groningen Oosterpoort, Holland
27.10.83 London Camden Electric Ballroom, England
28.10.83 London Imperial College S.U., England
29.10.83 Reading University, England
09.12.83 Vaals Spuugh, Holland
10.12.83 Amsterdam Meervaart, Holland

11.12.03 Den Bosch Casino, Holland
10.12.83 *BBC Radio 1 "In Concert" (Broadcast Date - not live)*
11.12.83 Den Bosch Casino, Holland

1984
23.04.84 Utrecht Vrije Vloer, Holland
24.04.84 Köln, Alter Wartesaal, West Germany
25.04.84 Hamburg Markthalle, West Germany
27.04.84 Bochum Zeche, Holland
??.10.84 Sheffield University, England

1985
24.08.85 London Crystal Palace Concert Bowl, England (Anti-Heroin
Campaign Benefit Festival)
29.09.85 Sheffield Limit Club, England
30.09.85 London Marquee, England
09.11.85 St. Andrews University, Fife, Scotland
15.11.85 London University Of London Union, England
29.11.85 Sheffield Limit Club, England
21.11.85 Utrecht Tivoli, Holland
22.11.85 Den Haag Paard van Troje, Holland
23.11.85 Haarlem Patronaat, Holland
24.11.85 Zaandam Drieluik, Holland
25.11.85 Groningen Oosterpoort, Holland
26.11.85 Amsterdam Paradiso, Holland
27.11.85 Wageningen Junushof, Holland
28.11.85 Leeuwarden Harmonie, Holland
29.11.85 Rotterdam Arena, Holland
30.11.85 Noord Scharwoude De Koog, Holland
05.12.85 London Marquee, England

1986
31.01.86 Suburbia, Perugia Italy
??.05.86 Amsterdam Paradiso, Holland

1987
22.01.87 Detmold The Hunky Dory Music Hall, West Germany
25.01.87 Hamburg Knopfs Music, West Germany
30.01.87 Vaals Spuugh, Holland
01.02.87 Amsterdam Paradiso, Holland
03.02.87 Rotterdam Lantaren, Holland
09.02.87 London, The Boston Arms, England
??.??.87 Bergen Hulen, Norway (underground air shelter!)
25.02.87 Madrid Astoria, Spain
26.02.87 Barcelona Zeleste, Spain
06.03.87 Salford University, England
11.03.87 Leeds Irish Centre, England

12.03.87 Bristol Polytechnic, England
13.03.87 Uxbridge Brunel University, England
14.03.87 Coventry Polytechnic, England
19.03.87 Edinburgh The Venue, Scotland
20.03.87 Glasgow University Queen Margaret Union, Scotland
21.03.87 Aberdeen The Venue, Scotland
28.04.87 Montreal Le Spectrum, Canada
??.04.87 Carleton University Porter Hall, Ottawa, Canada
??.04.87 Toronto Concert Hall, Canada
13.05.87 Philadelphia Chesnut Cabaret, USA
??.05.87 Pittsburgh Grafitti Club, USA
??.05.87 Memphis The Antenna, USA
??.05.87 New Orleans Tipatina's or Jimmy's, USA
??.05.87 Los Angeles Variety Arts Theatre, USA
??.05.87 New York, USA
??.05.87 Amsterdam Paradiso, Holland
15.08.87 Waterpop Festival, Wateringen, Holland
00.00.87 The Tube Channel 4 TV Newcastle, England

1992
29.06.92 Sheffield University Union, The Park, England
??.07.92 Sheffield City Hall Ballroom, England
??.07.92 Sheffield Festival Zap Tent, England
17.07.92 Manchester International, England
??.10.92 Hull Adelphi, England
30.10.92 London Mean Fiddler, England

1993
15.01.93 London Mean Fiddler, England
22.01.93 Manchester Underground UMIST, England
26.01.93 Arnhem Willemeen, Holland
27.01.93 Groningen Simplon, Holland
28.01.93 Amsterdam Paradiso, Holland
29.01.93 Deventer Burgerweeshuis, Holland
30.01.93 KRO Hilversum, Holland
31.01.93 Brussels VK, Belgium
03.02.93 Utrecht Vrije Vloer, Holland
04.02.93 Hanover Fluhzirkus, Germany
05.02.93 Krefeld Kulturfabrik, Germany
06.02.93 Wilhelmshaven Pumpwerk, Germany
07.02.93 Hamburg Soundgarden, Germany
08.02.93 Detmold Hunk Dory, Germany
09.02.93 Saarbrucken Ballhaus, Germany
10.02.93 Munster Subway, Germany
11.02.93 Giessen Club Bizarre, Germany
12.02.93 Den Haag Paard Van Troje, Holland

13.02.93 Uden Nieuwe Pul, Holland
14.02.93 Leiden LVC, Holland
17.02.93 Stuttgart, Germany
18.02.93 Heidelberg Schwimmbad, Germany
19.02.93 Nurnberg Komm, Germany
20.02.93 Berlin Knaack Club, Germany
21.02.93 Magdeburg TV Show, Germany
05.03.93 London Venue, England
23.06.93 London Camden Underworld, England
25.06.93 Leeds Duchess Of York, England
26.06.93 Glasgow King Tut's Wah Wah Hut, Scotland
28.06.93 Stoke Wheatsheaf, England
30.06.93 Buckley Tivoli Ballroom, England
01.07.93 Leicester Princess Charlotte, England
03.07.93 Reading After Dark, England
??.07/93 Birmingham, England
??.07/93 Liverpool, England
06.08.93 Vlissingen Bellamypark, Holland
07.08.93 Hoogkarspel Rhythm & Blues Festival, Holland
08.08.93 Amsterdam Sleepin/Arena, Holland
14.08.93 Reading After Dark, England
01.10.93 Oss Papillon, Holland
02.10.93 Bliksem Brummen, Holland
03.10.93 Hoorn Troll, Holland
05.10.93 Brussels Ancienne Belgique Luna Theatre, Belgium
07.10.93 Enschede Atak, Holland
08.10.93 Vaals Spuugh, Holland
09.10.93 Dordrecht Bibelot, Holland
10.10.93 Eindhoven Altstadt, Holland
15.10.93 Zaandam Drieluik, Holland
16.10.93 Zwolle Hedon, Holland
17.10.93 Baarloo Sjiwa, Holland
21.10.93 Heiloo Buk Buk, Holland
22.10.93 De Meern Azotod, Holland
23.10.93 Wateringen Nederland 3, Holland
27.10.93 Bergen Op Zoom Botte Hommel, Holland
28.10.93 Zoetermeer Boerderij, Holland
29.10.93 Heemskerk Donkey Shot, Holland
30.10.93 Lichtenvoorde Kei-festival, Holland
25.11.93 BBC Radio 1, England, Guest List with Mark Kermode

1994
04.03.94 Silvolde Pan, Holland
05.03.94 Purmerend Kern, Holland
06.03.94 Emmen Brasserie, Holland
07.03.94 Groningen De Kar, Holland
08.03.94 Amsterdam Naar Boven, Holland

10.03.94 Rotterdam Out of Time, Holland
11.03.94 Uden Nieuwe Pul, Holland
12.03.94 Heino Struik, Holland

1995
28.06.95 Sheffield University Union, The Park, England
30.06.95 London Mean Fiddler, England
03.07.95 York Fibbers, England
05.07.95 Hull Adelphi, England
06.07.95 Leeds Duchess Of York, England
11.07.95 Liverpool The Lomax, England
12.07.95 Bristol Fleece & Firkin, England
13.07.95 Swindon The Venue Monkey Club, England

2009 Re-union Gigs
27.04.09 O2 Academy, Sheffield, England (the original line-up played at this gig)
22.10.09 Glasgow ABC, Scotland
23.10.09 Manchester Academy, England
24.10.09 London Academy (Islington), England
11.12.10 The Plug, Sheffield, England

Appendix 1

The Comsat Angels – Manchester Academy 3, Friday 23-10-2009

This concert marked a milestone as, possibly, the penultimate appearance of The Comsat Angels. I sensed a certain sadness with this in mind as the band took to the stage.

Opening with the haunting 'Sleep No More' followed by the strident 'Be Brave', both from the band's second album Sleep No More, it was apparent that the previous night's concert in Glasgow had prepared them for what was likely to be a memorable event.

Songs such as 'Missing in Action' and 'Independence Day' were clearly audience pleasers, but it was the more recent material such as 'I Hear a New World', from the most recent studio album The Glamour, which placed the band's ever-developing sound world in context. This was somehow prophetic in tone considering the path that, for example, vocalist/guitarist Stephen Fellows is likely to take in the future. With the absence of original bassist Kevin Bacon, replaced by Terry Todd, the band's emphasis on their more recent repertoire seemed to grow in relevance throughout the performance. It proved one thing: the band were as relevant during the 1990s as they were in the 1980s and, if they were to continue, would undoubtedly adapt to current styles. 'Postcard', from the first album Waiting for a Miracle, was as powerful as during the first come-back performance the band played in Sheffield earlier this year.

The first encore brought the brooding 'Valley of the Nile' – again from the much-underrated The Glamour (possibly one of the best albums of the 1990s) – and with the band returning for a second time, 'Driving' from My Mind's Eye, took on a life of its own. It's clear from this song where bands such as The Foo Fighters have turned for inspiration with the chugging added-note chords in the guitar part. It was also interesting to hear 'The Cutting Edge' from the late '80s Island album Chasing Shadows taking the band into, as Stephen Fellows commented, 'jazz territory'.

Fellows's final comment seemed to sum-up the evening: 'The NME have referred to us for this tour as a "veteran Indie band".' Personally, I still have the original NME clipping of the first review of Independence Day on the original single I bought at the time. My thoughts ran something like this: 'how time flies.' But then I thought, 'Hang on. The Comsats started all this. Veteran? It must be prime-movers!' As Fellows subsequently commented, 'People change the facts to fit the story.'

Andrew Keeling. 24-10-2009.

The Comsat Angels

O2 Academy, Sheffield

26th April 2009

Comsat Angels- The O2 in London Oct 2009
Photo © Jan Todd

Last Weekend Tour London O2
Photo © Jan Todd

Comsat Angels' rehearsal April 8th 2009
Photo © Jan Todd

Comsat Angels' rehearsal 26th November 2010
Photo © Jan Todd

Comsat Christmas! Andy,Kev,Mik, Terry after gig drink
Photo © Jan Todd

Appendix 2

Three songs transcribed into score from Comsat Angels' albums Sleep No More (Sleep No More and Gone) and My Mind's Eye (Shiva Descending).

6.

Appendix 3

Nick Robinson – My Involvement with the Comsat Angels

(Nick Robinson's essay is included from an insider/outsider view of the Comsat Angels.)

My involvement with the Comsats began early. As a local musician, I always took a keen interest in the 'opposition', to see how my band/s compared and what I could learn from them. Amongst these was a band called Xero, featuring future Comsat Terry Todd. Another was called The Extras with future Comsat Simon Anderson.

I first saw The Comsat Angels at the Broadfield, my local pub (which provided a much needed stage for new bands) on 07/07/79. They were new and strange to my ears. Coming from a rock/prog background, I found the sparse quality of their songs and Steve's guitar-work intriguing and inspiring. At this time I joined up with some local musicians to form Active Gliders who progressed to become Red Zoo. Our singer, Elaine, was living with Kevin Bacon at the time, so it was only natural we began to follow them around and play the odd support slot. Kevin Bacon also produced our first proper demos (and opened various doors) which resulted in a deal with Polydor, sharing the Comsats' Swingbest management company.

The Comsats (or The Sitcoms, as a lot of people locally

affectionately called them) kindly offered us the chance to re-record a cover of their first single 'Ring Ring, Shrink Shrink', an idea which we liked but our manager promptly rejected. Kevin produced more demos of our songs and so he got see and hear my guitar playing quite a bit. We shared an obsession with music equipment, so I'd be listening to him explain the Dolby system long after the others had fallen asleep. He told me stories from the life of the band and they would play me unreleased demos/songs and explain all the problems with the mix. One such was listening to the beautiful 'Pray for Rain', where Andy pointed out that the 'guide piano' could still be heard towards the end. Another was with tracks from 7 Day Weekend, where I'd say "I love this song" and Andy would rightly complain "Me and Mik aren't on it!" This was the Jive era were the label was desperate to have the band 'fit in' with the fashion of the day, including drum machines!

Mik was the same full-on person I know and love today, although back then, he could sustain it for longer. A superb drummer, I loved how he would consistently find unusual yet musical patterns to play. I shared his delight with the drum sound on Sleep No More, recorded in a lift-shaft! Steve was (and remains) a highly reclusive personality, cursed with the inability to accept what talent he has. We talked from time to time, but Mik and Andy were certainly the two most down-to-earth in the band.

I was approached by the band to play guitar for them around the summer of 1987. Kev had previously made subtle enquiries about what kind of guitar styles I could play and it was clear they were sounding me out, but frustratingly in the past they went for someone else. This time it was for real, so we started rehearsing at their room (one of the many old redundant cutlery workshops which were home to nearly all Sheffield bands at one time or another). Steve felt my equipment "wasn't up to it", so he lent me a gold Strat and a Marshall 50 watt combo. Although I'd played with many bands prior to this, it was a pure pleasure to actually play in one of my favourite bands. The volume, intensity and passion were of a level I hadn't experienced before and to play with a drummer like Mik was a real revelation.

At this stage the band had changed their name to Dream Command, having originally thought about becoming The Headhunters. The name change was due to objections from an

American company with the glorious name of The Communications Satellite Inc (aka the ComSat Corporation). Someone from the company sent the band's manager a list of proposed dates for their US tour which were not even public at the time, and they suspected someone was hacking into his computer from a high level. This and a plan to relaunch their career post-Polydor led to the name change. Island were really keen on the band and much was promised.

The idea of me joining was, as in the past, to take the guitar weight from Steve's shoulders for a forthcoming tour of America, so that he could concentrate on his singing. I didn't really think he needed any help, but kept this to myself. We rehearsed songs from what was to become the Dream Command album. I'm a fast learner, so we didn't use chord sheets. I picked it up from various demo cassettes. One particular highlight was playing 'Something's Got to Give', the b-side of the 'Cutting Edge' 45. That I'd been in love with since I first heard it. The fact that I got to do the fabulous solo at the end was almost too good to be true.

So, all rehearsed, we played a pre-tour gig at a small out-of-town Sheffield music venue called 'Take 2'. The gig itself went well and, as it turned out, was my first and last gig with the band. The US arm of Island funding the tour decided there were no hit singles on the Fire on the Moon album, so pulled the plug on the tour and told them to write something more commercial!

The tour being delayed, the band told me there was little point rehearsing, they would wait for Steve to write a hit single, then get me back onboard when the tour was re-scheduled. Disappointed but still optimistic, I waited for the call. When it came, I didn't expect it to be in a local music shop, where I struck up conversation with someone admiring the Fender section. "Do you play with anyone?" I asked. "Yes", came the reply, "the Comsat Angels, I'm going to do a US tour with them". This unlikely coincidence worried me and a quick call to Andy confirmed my worst fears.

I never did hear a reason why they had made this choice, but essentially Steve and Kev had pushed it through against the wishes of the other two, who (all credit to them) were highly embarrassed. Maybe they found someone with more technique; more fashion sense. I never found out, because they abandoned plans to expand in the end and went back to being a four-piece. I suspect my familiarity with them encouraged me to behave as if I was part of the future of the band rather just than a hired hand, but I've always had difficulty keeping my opinions to myself. Perhaps I was just too eager!

Years passed, Mik and Andy came to see me play with my subsequent bands and we remained friends. Kev decided to quit playing in bands and touring to further his career as a producer of some reputation. My brother Simon was running RPM Records by this time and, after engineering a detailed series of CDs of the band's original albums, set about releasing the upcoming new CD My Mind's Eye (on Thunderbird Records). Despite this being a powerful album, success once again eluded them.

The band followed this with the even more remarkable The Glamour album but a subsequent tour proved to be so badly organised that in Manchester posters were still being slapped up round the venue as the band arrived for the rehearsal (with fellow Sheffield guitarist Richard Hawley along for the ride). Faced with half a dozen people, the band thought 'fuck it' and stormed through a set anyway – only for the hall manager to come on near the end and turn the power off. You can hardly blame them for knocking it on the head.

I went for some jams with Mik and Andy's follow-up band Soup (I'm delighted that the recordings they made are now finally available via download). I saw Steve most often in Record Collector, Sheffield's famous indie store, where he worked part-time for a while in the vinyl department. It was here that he heard the demos of a new band called Gomez, a group he went on to manage for several years. Steve introduced me to the work of David Torn, who has been a huge influence since.

Steve recorded a solo instrumental CD, Mood X in 1987, released by an offshoot of RPM, English Electric. He'd been recording demos at drummer Rod Siddal's mini-studio, which happened to be next door to where my mum lived. So, every time I saw mum, I'd pop next door. At one point he even came round to my house where we began briefly to work on some new material together. Over the years, Steve has recorded probably hundreds of demos, but few seem to live up to his demands and expectations, so simply gather dust on his shelves. More recently, he has released some of these through his Myspace page, proving once again the depth of his musical gifts (if not social networking trends!). One, called 'Evening Air', is as good as anything he's ever recorded.

I've followed the band's career with keen interest since the start. However briefly our paths crossed, their music is a fundamental a part of my adult life. It's a salutary lesson that these guys spent most of their musical lives together, made some stunning music, yet have little to show for it (certainly not money) apart from a growing and long overdue public recognition of how special they were. This prompted a few local reunion shows for the annual Sensoria music and media industry event and beyond, but seems unlikely to be repeated.

I have sporadic contact with Kev but see little of Steve, although I live in hope he will overcome his doubts and release some fresh music before much longer. More recently I've been having irregular jams with Mik and Andy in their little practice space at Neepsend. Once with Terry Todd on bass, on other occasions with a superb jazz bassist called John Prideaux. Essentially evenings of what could loosely be described as 'instrumental jazz rock', they have been some of the most rewarding sessions I've had in my life.

All in all, I'm proud I had my brief time with them. In a sad, selfish way it proves to me that I did have what it took and I still love and play their music often. In some ways, I'm almost pleased not to have achieved the same level of success. To have left behind such a catalogue of breath-taking music and not have a penny-piece to show for it must leave a feeling of deep regret. However, they have left a musical legacy that remains influential, respected and loved around the world (just witness the pan-European crowd who packed the front rows for those reunion shows). Offered that at the outset, most of us would surely settle for it.

About the Author

Andrew Keeling is a composer and musician living in the North of England and has a PhD from the University of Manchester.

He has a particular interest in the music of King Crimson and has written four Musical Guides on the band's music. He has also orchestrated the Soundscapes of Robert Fripp which have been performed in concert and appeared on the DGM/Panegyric CD 'The Wine of Silence', received to widespread critical acclaim.

As a flautist, he has formed an improvisation duo with former King Crimson violinist David Cross.

Andrew Keeling & Otherword (A. K., Stephen Fellows etc.) have released Bells of Heaven, Hyde and My Red Book (Spaceward Records).

Also available from Spaceward

Also by Andrew Keeling

Musical Guide to In The Court Of The Crimson King by King
Crimson
(ISBN 978-0-9562977-0-9)

~

Musical Guide to In The Wake Of Poseidon by King Crimson and
McDonald and Giles by McDonald and Giles
(ISBN 978-0-9562977-1-6)

~

Musical Guide to Larks' Tongues In Aspic by King Crimson
(ISBN 978-0-9562977-2-3)

~

The Concise Musical Guide to King Crimson and Robert Fripp
(1969 - 1984)
(ISBN 978-0-9570489-3-5)

~

In the Shadow - Glimpsing the Creative Unconscious
Volume 1 - The DGM Diaries (1999 - 2001)
(ISBN 978-0-9562977-3-0)

~

In the Shadow - Glimpsing the Creative Unconscious
Volume 2 - The FraKctured Zone Diaries (2006 - 2012)
(ISBN 978-0-9562977-3-5)

~